Growing Food in a Short Season

Growing Food in a Short Season

SUSTAINABLE, ORGANIC COLD-CLIMATE GARDENING

MELANIE J. WATTS

Douglas & McIntyre

Douglas and McIntyre (2013) Ltd.
P.O. Box 219
Madeira Park, BC, Canada V0N 2H0
www.douglas-mcintyre.com

Edited by Carol Pope
Index by Stephen Ullstrom
Cover design by Diane Robertson
Text design by Roger Handling

Additional Photo Credits: p.16 *bhpfack2/Thinkstock*; p.89, 140 *Martin Poole/Thinkstock*; p.141 *Rajinder Mudhar/Thinkstock*; p.142 *mira33/Thinkstock*; p.143 (right) *IngridHS/Thinkstock*; p.143 (bottom) *Monkey Business Images/Thinkstock*; p.144 *Marlene Ford/Thinkstock*; p. 152 *Therion256/Thinkstock*; p.153 *aksenya/Thinkstock*; p.158 *Olena Mykhaylova/Thinkstock*; p.159 *arihen/Thinkstock*; p.164 *Robert M Peacock/Thinkstock*; p.165 *tycoon751/Thinkstock*; p.166 *Jack Jelly/Thinkstock*; p.168 *M Kucova/Thinkstock*; p.171 *livcool/Thinkstock*. Colour insert: pages i–v Christina Symons, vi (top) *Celena Beech/Thinkstock*; vi (bottom) *Anthony Jones/Thinkstock*. Cover photo credits: front top *Diana Taliun/Thinkstock*; front left *Dusko Kostic/Thinkstock*; front middle *dmitrii_designer/Thinkstock*; front right *sanddebeautheil/Thinkstock*; back middle *audaxl/Thinkstock*; back right *M Kucova/Thinkstock*; back bottom *Trinette Reed/Stocksy United;* endsheets *tom-iuchenko/Thinkstock*.

Printed and bound in Canada

Canada Council   Conseil des Arts
for the Arts   du Canada

BRITISH COLUMBIA
ARTS COUNCIL
An agency of the Province of British Columbia

We gratefully acknowledge financial support from the Government of Canada through the Canada Book Fund and the Canada Council for the Arts, and from the Province of British Columbia through the BC Arts Council and the Book Publishing Tax Credit.

Cataloguing data available from Library and Archives Canada
978-1-77162-011-6 (paper)
978-1-77162-012-3 (ebook)

ACKNOWLEDGEMENTS

This book is for my mother and father, who taught me to love what I have, celebrate the earth and appreciate differences in others.

Many thanks to Carol Pope, my editor, for noticing my enthusiastic postings on my blog, *northerngardenersalmanac.com*, and encouraging me to write this book. Thanks, Carol, for your patience, help and guidance.

A huge shout out and a pickup load of thanks to my friends and neighbours in Tomslake, Tupper and Dawson Creek. Everything I know about farming and neighbourliness I learned from you. Some of my most treasured memories are from the great times I had while living in the BC Peace.

And a special thanks to these friends:

Hillary, who taught me to leave root crops in the ground to overwinter for harvest the following spring.

Susannah, for sending me photos of 'Dwarf Blue Scotch' kale that regrew in her Prince George garden.

Marguerite, for gifting me many varieties of heirloom tomato seeds for my collection and experimentation.

Gayla, for gifting me Jerusalem artichoke tubers and allowing me to appropriate her knowledge of redefining radish greens and frosted overripe lettuce as edible food.

And to:

Harrowsmith magazine and the many *Harrowsmith* gardening books, for inspiring me and giving me the confidence many years ago to pick up a spade and plant my first seed.

CONTENTS

PREFACE

*A*s a garden-magazine editor for more than a decade, I had my sources of inspiration—bloggers and writers I would check in with regularly to gather momentum and build up knowledge of what was going on in gardens around the country. One blogger who never failed to inspire me with both her cheerful common sense and impressive results was Melanie Watts. Her steady stream of stories from her prolific vegetable patch and orchard, along with well-honed advice on growing food in harmony with nature, was both motivating and enticing. And impressive as Melanie's garden blog was, it was 10 times more so when one took into account that she was talking to us from zones 2 and 3—among the coldest possible in North America.

Despite several feet of snow piled over her garden September through May, Melanie has grown enough food for the last 25 years to sustain herself and her family with vegetables and fruits through the summer months, plus stock her cold room and freezer for the lengthy winter. And she makes it all sound easy.

Determined to enjoy the short but spectacular northern growing season rather than spend it in the kitchen, Melanie savours fast and fresh fare throughout the warm days, plucking petals and produce for flower salads, veggie barbecues, bitter-green stir-fries, fresh-herb teas and infused oils and vinegars—and embracing every possible moment in the sunshine. Summer produce is quickly and efficiently stored to be roasted, stewed and nibbled during the long, chilly winter. Herbs and tomatoes are dried, fruits and greens frozen, pestos bottled, cabbage fermented, and root vegetables and garlic cured and heaped into cold storage. In fall and winter, Late-Harvest Ratatouille and Pureed Beet Soup warm home and hearth.

Back in the garden, while the spring season arrives only after a lengthy ebb and flow of freezing and thawing, Melanie has figured out every trick to hurry the harvest—from earmarking microclimates to rigging up heat boosters using recycled materials.

Melanie's garden hums with bees and beneficial insects, thanks to her gentle touch that lets nature do most of the work. Good weeds are welcomed, clay soil is enriched by strategies that encourage earth's helpful organisms to do the manual labour, and a wide spectrum of plant life is nurtured with healthy diversity as the ultimate objective.

With an extensive listing of cold-hardy food plants arranged by plant family to help with planning crop rotation—key to growing a pest-resistant organic food garden—this book guides the cold-climate gardener down the path to an abundant harvest and increased sustainability despite challenging climate conditions and a sometimes seemingly relentless winter.

Carol Pope
Garden Editor

The Cultivation of a Food Gardener

IN THE NORTH, SUMMER IS A BRIEF RESPITE BETWEEN FROSTS... NEVERTHELESS, GARDENING IS WHAT I DO

The calendar said April but the world was still covered in white. We stepped out of the car onto a snowy field. My husband hoisted the baby into his arms and I zipped up my coat, jammed a toque down low over my ears and tried to avoid loving licks from a giant dog that appeared the instant the car engine was turned off.

We heard a shout and turned our heads. A man stood on the deck of a snow-cocooned house. It was a nice home, made of logs, hunkered down at the back of the field, on the south side of acres and acres of poplar and spruce trees, also covered in snow.

I wanted this. Not so much this place but the chance to live off the land, to grow my own food. Since childhood, perhaps spurred by Laura Ingalls Wilder's Little House books, I've been obsessed with a compelling fervour, an overwhelming desire, to do things for myself.

We bought the place.

Never mind that it was 50 kilometres from the nearest town. Never mind that the land was in the Peace River country, a place on the distant northeastern edge of British Columbia, far away from civilization as we knew it. Never mind (as I found out later) that the area possessed such an unforgiving climate that the Canadian government rated it to be in plant hardiness zone 2. Such an evaluation is based on the ability of the area's plants to endure months of severe, persistent, freezing, icy weather. The coldest plant hardiness zone in Canada is rated 0 and the mildest 9.

There's an enormous barn and a garden patch that the man assures us has been recently manured. A dilapidated, rusted machine called a rototiller stands on the edge of the garden. Down one side of the house, several cords of wood are stacked like a wall. The owner of the house generously donates his axe—he has no further use for it.

It's spring and the snow is melting, collecting into a puddle that grows bigger every day in front of the house. As the frost comes out of the ground, the driveway turns to mud, thick and slimy like peanut butter. It sticks to my city shoes in lumps so

Our first home in the BC Peace.

that they become heavier with each step. The car does even worse, and after spending hours one Saturday extracting it from the long driveway, we start parking it up by the road. Every day—carrying the toddler with one arm, grocery bag with the other—we're forced to make our slippery way slowly down the long driveway to the house.

At the end of the summer, I give birth to our second child. The days get darker, the ground freezes and snow smothers the land around the house. I take to reading gardening books while sitting on the couch breastfeeding. One book, *Harrowsmith Northern Gardener*, seems like it was written for me.

By the time the calendar rolls around to June, the baby is outside crawling in the first blades of grass, watched over by the critical eye of the toddler, and I'm anxiously checking the calendar, waiting for the date of the last frost to come and go so that I can safely plant out my precious seedlings. The summer is hot and the garden grows magnificently. I'm awed when I harvest the vegetables, marvelling at their perfect shapes, just like the ones from the supermarket, and exclaiming over their exquisite taste, better than the ones from the supermarket.

I staked the tomatoes as instructed, so they grow tall, healthy, and bear a large crop of green tomatoes. I start listening to the weather forecasts and scrutinizing the thermometer before bed, wondering if there will be a frost. My gardening book warns that the first fall frosts are likely to strike any time after the second week of August. I'm torn because I want to leave them on the vine long enough to ripen but not so long they are killed.

When I planted that first garden, I was following a dream: to live on the land lightly, paying attention to the cycles of weather and time, working towards self-sufficiency in vegetables.

We bought sheep for the barn. Part of me wanted to get chickens, even a milk cow, but reality—in the form of a husband with a government job that kept him away from the farm five days a week—left me knowing I would be alone with the two children to pursue my passion. I decided bringing up the children, growing vegetables and raising sheep was enough. Besides, they were all tasks I knew little about. As my flock expanded, my knowledge of gardening, animal husbandry and how to work the land grew. I began to call myself a sheep farmer.

Since those long-ago halcyon days, I've planted thousands of seeds, designed and created three gardens, and acquired a vast repository of experience and knowledge about raising food crops, flowers, sheep and children in the cold climate of the north.

The Role of Manure

Way back in 1971, Frances Moore Lappé wrote in her book *Diet for a Small Planet* that it takes more land to raise protein in the form of a cow than it does to raise vegetable protein in the form of beans and grains: the protein production ratio is 21–1. She explained that a cow must be fed 21 pounds of protein to produce 1 pound of protein for human consumption. When I read this in the early 1980s, I felt guilty that so much land was being used to produce meat for my hamburgers.

Today, most animals raised for meat end their lives in feedlots, where they are fed large quantities of grain to get them to market weight. Lappé says this is unnecessary and an incredible waste of protein. She says ruminants like cattle and sheep can convert nitrogen in their stomachs into protein.

Prior to modern farming, animal wastes were put back onto the fields to build the soil and provide fertilizer for plants. Nowadays, chemical fertilizers feed plants while animal wastes are unused. Manure builds up in huge piles. Runoff from the waste pollutes the water supply. In the BC Peace, I saw many lakes clogged with algae blooms due to the excessive amounts of nitrogen washing into them from surrounding farms.

On my homestead, the sheep filled a vital niche that perfectly complemented all

My sheep farm at the beginning of winter.

the other aspects of the farm, including the pastures, compost bins, and food and flower gardens. Their manure was piled into a corner of the paddock. In the spring, the oldest pile was spread onto the gardens. Sheep manure is a plentiful supply of plant nutrition, promoting soil health by encouraging worms and microorganisms to congregate beneath it to digest and break it down into a form of nutrition the plants use to grow.

Manure production is a positive side effect of raising animals—it feeds the soil that in turn feeds the plants, and it's free.

Because manure is so useful in feeding the soil, raising animals is a necessary component of the new, sustainable, mixed farm. Eating meat a few times a week from grass-fed animals, where their by-products are part of the farming cycle, helps the earth. Using manure rather than chemical fertilizers ensures that the soil is alive, full of microbes, bacteria, insects and worms. Soil that is alive grows healthy plants that are better able to resist disease. Such plants are chock full of nutrients that humans and animals can use when we eat them. Incorporating small amounts of meat into our diet provides necessary nutrients, amino acids and iron in quantities not found in other foods. Animals allowed to roam fields have more muscle. Meat from these animals is leaner and tastes better than factory-raised meat.

Many cities allow homeowners to raise chickens in their backyards, although for those unable to do this it is easy enough to seek out farmers who are raising animals sustainably. Farm markets, health-food stores and Internet searching are ways to find farmers who will sell you grass-fed meat and free-range chickens. Ask them how they raise their animals and what they feed them. Buying meat directly from farmers gives you peace of mind; it tastes better than factory-produced meat, and it's sometimes even cheaper and supports a growing local network of sustainable farms.

Ask the same farmers for manure. Chances are they have more than they need and are happy to let you take some away for free.

Why Grow Food Organically?

Another problem with modern farming, says Lappé, is that residues from chemical fertilizers, herbicides and pesticides accumulate in food. These deposits become more concentrated as you move up the food chain. While vegetables have relatively little concentration of toxins, animals that eat those vegetables retain more, and humans at the top of the food chain have the highest level of toxic-residue accumulation.

Lappé's assertion that toxins from chemical herbicides, pesticides and fertilizers accumulate in the food chain convinced me to garden organically. I joined The Peace River Organic Producers Association (PROPA) to learn more.

Around that time, in the late 1980s and early 1990s, mainstream awareness was building around the idea that human activities had a negative effect on Earth. This idea spurred the beginnings of the popular "Green" movement. Organic food and ways to grow organic food became front-page news. Suddenly organic herbicides, pesticides and fertilizers were for sale on the shelves of garden centres and hardware stores.

Sustainability?

It was 1992 and environmentalists from everywhere were meeting in Rio de Janeiro for the United Nations Conference on Environment and Development (Earth Summit). Headlines screamed the message that the world as we knew it would be fast disappearing unless we did something to save what was left of it.

Back on the farm, I joined the local recycling group. I took my young children with me when I went to the grocery store to tell the manager I didn't want to buy meat on a Styrofoam tray wrapped in plastic.

I knew that what I was doing on the farm was right. Although back then the word "sustainability" was not part of my narrative, using sheep's waste to grow food was in fact all about sustainability.

Is Local Food Better?

A decade later, a new movement called "Local Food" vied for our attention. We became aware that our food production was becoming increasingly centralized in faraway places where the climate is warm enough to grow crops year-round.

Words like "locavore" and concepts like "open-pollinated" and "heirloom" seed entered our lexicon, along with the scary "genetically modified organism (GMO)."

The distance that food travels to our plates is only one part of the equation. Buying tomatoes or cucumbers from a local grower may not be better if they are grown in a heated greenhouse with artificial lighting. As carbon-footprint expert Mike Berners-Lee points out, food that is ripened using energy from the sun is always a better choice.

Farming Badly

For me, it started with an old *Harrowsmith* article that suggested farming badly was better: it was less work, saved energy and, without the need for the latest farm machinery or gadget, was cheaper. Reading this, I had difficulty grasping the concept and understanding how it would apply to gardening.

And I was distracted by another topic: soil. I knew earthworms were good because they burrowed around in it, fluffing it up, making it lighter and easier for microbes and plant roots to flourish.

In the spring, when I took apart my compost heap there were always lots of wiggly worms in it. When I put the compost on the garden, the worms were added too. I suspected they had a role in helping to break down the organic matter in the pile.

One year, the compost pile was taken over by ants. At a loss as to how to get rid of them, I let them stay. Later, I was gratified when I noticed they did an even better job of breaking down the organic matter than the worms did.

Through reading, I learned that orchids—the hardy native ones that grow in northern BC, like *Calypso bulbosa*, *Cypripedium montanum* and others—have an established relationship between their roots and fungi in the soil. This relationship makes it difficult to transplant wild orchids. Leave them where you find them. I later learned that fungi and mycorrhizae have an impact in my food garden too.

Years later, in my third garden, I decided to plant a clover lawn around my new

house. Clover roots grow down deeper than grass roots, so I reasoned I would not need to water. Clover fixes nitrogen, making its own food, so I reasoned I would not need to fertilize. If I planted Dutch white clover (*Trifolium repens*), which reaches only a few centimetres high, I would not have to mow. I bought the seed. The first year, it grew into an exuberant green lawn humming with bees, another bonus. In succeeding years, it started to die out in low spots; I reseeded these areas, but native species moved in, growing faster than the clover and colonizing these areas.

My now-weedy clover lawn has attracted an increased variety of insects and microorganisms. I'm sure this expanded diversity is why I've yet to have major problems with insects or disease interfering with my garden plants. Because I let nature, for the most part, plant the lawn around my house, I never need to water, fertilize or mow it. I use the weed whacker to clear away the luxuriant growth just before the plants go to seed.

Left: The clover/weed lawn around my house and garden.

Above right: Farm badly by letting your plants go to seed—these radish flowers attract bugs good and bad into my garden.

Working with Nature

Gardening is not a battle with nature to try to tame it and make it do our bidding. Nobody cultivates the forest or grasslands—these ecosystems do fine without us. Learning to work with nature is an easy, wise, practical and sensible approach to gardening.

Working with nature entails that you pay attention to the seasons and the cycles of day and night, and how they affect the weather and plant growth. Watch what happens when you clear away vegetation, exposing the soil. What weeds move in first, what shrubs establish next? I saw nature in action when I tried to grow a mono-crop of clover.

The next time you get a bug infestation, let nature deal with it. The garden of my second house, in the city, was constantly invaded by swarms of different species of aphids, caterpillars and other less-familiar bugs. I spent days trying to wash the aphids off the trees, pick the caterpillars off the roses and wipe away all the other insects. After a couple years of dragging my fingernails across the blackboard, despite my interfering, nature was able to rebalance the garden's ecosystem and the annoying bugs left.

I'm sure the many varieties of perennial flowers, shrubs, herbs and vegetables I added attracted an assortment of beneficial insects and microorganisms. Not spraying chemicals to get rid of the bugs, and spreading generous applications of compost and manure onto the gardens helped too.

Real Food

All it takes to produce real food in your own garden is healthy soil, sunlight and water. Building up the soil is a vital first step towards growing tasty, nutritious, real food. As author and activist Michael Pollan points out, the most flavourful food is easily recognizable as itself, requires the least ingredients and is fresh.

Vegetables grown in my garden travel mere metres to my plate. Sometimes I linger in the greenhouse, pulling warm, red tomatoes off the vine. Juice squirts onto my chin as I bite into one and grab a leaf from the basil plant growing beneath the vine—its deep, rich taste is the perfect complement to the sweetness of the fresh tomato.

The juicy benefits of growing your own.

All winter, I look forward to the first bite of sorrel, a perennial herb that resurfaces in the garden soon after the snow melts: its acidic, crisp, slightly sour-tasting leaves wake up my taste buds, priming them for the all-too-short season of fresh garden produce ahead.

Vegetables as fresh as these need no flavour add-ons, beyond a simple shake of salt, a grinding of pepper, perhaps a glug of olive oil.

Cooking food deepens the flavours, increasing its complexity. Slow-roasting root vegetables caramelizes natural sugars, upping the taste meter tenfold.

For most of the year, the northern garden is buried beneath snow. Plants lie dormant, waiting for the land to thaw so they can start growing again. During this time, I switch my focus from eating fresh-from-the-garden vegetables and fruit to those easily stored in the root cellar— carrots, cabbage, beets, potatoes and apples—and those that keep well when frozen, dried or canned—tomatoes, peas, beans, greens like kale, Swiss chard, collard greens, spinach, berry and tree fruits. After all, who craves a lettuce salad when outside it's a frigid -10C and snowing heavily?

By growing my own food, I choose the varieties I like, garden organically, and have fun doing it. I've harvested buckets and buckets of satisfaction from planting seeds, nurturing the plants, watching them grow, harvesting and finally enjoying the delicious food. Eating at my house is like dining at an expensive luxury restaurant every day of the week. Actually, it's far superior—few of these restaurants have their own gardens seconds away from the kitchen.

Taking time to grow your own vegetables—whether in a few pots on your balcony, a plot in your community garden, or your front yard—is a rewarding experience. And, making it even better, the skills and knowledge you learn can be shared with your children.

When I started my farming career, I attended a weekend conference put on by the Peace River Organic Producers Association in Dawson Creek. The speaker who gave the keynote address was Dr. Stuart B. Hill, a scientist from McGill University. Since the early 1970s, he has believed that even though conventional agriculture's reliance on fossil fuel may feed more people than ever before, it is not sustainable. Organic—or ecological agriculture practised regionally—is healthier for the environment and better meets our nutritional needs.

At the time, his nonconformist views were received with suspicion. Ignoring the naysayers and those who thought he was crazy, he established Ecological Agricultural Projects (EAP) at McGill University, a source of information on ecological farming and gardening, renewable energy, rural development, nutrition and health.

I found his address inspirational, not only for its content on sustainable agriculture but because of his belief and unswerving conviction that his views, no matter how unconventional, were right.

At the end of his address, he said, "Don't try to change the world, because you can't—change yourself and the rest will follow." Those words have stuck with me ever since.

What I've Learned

- Eat small amounts of grass-fed meat that is grown by you or local farmers, remembering that animal wastes build up the earth in your garden, keeping soil healthy and alive.
- Grow your own "real" food, or buy it from people in your community who farm sustainably.
- "Farm badly" by letting nature work for you: welcome plant diversity and let sunshine and soil organisms decompose your compost and build up the soil.
- Let nature fight bug infestations and water your plants.
- Celebrate the sun. Its life-giving rays speed up decomposition, killing off unwanted fungi and mould. And sunshine is great for sterilizing anything (think diapers). It helps plants photosynthesize and produce oxygen, it helps us humans make vitamin D. A sunny day is the best kind of day.
- And, yes, you can grow food—enough to last January through to December— even if, like me, you live in a place where the ground is frozen and covered in snow for most of the year.

Get Ready to Grow

YES, YOU CAN GROW FOOD—ENOUGH TO LAST THROUGH THE YEAR—EVEN IF YOU LIVE WHERE THE GROUND IS FROZEN MOST OF THE TIME

Buried under all that snow are the roots of perennials, protected and dormant in their garden beds.

CHAPTER 1

A Healthy Start to a Sustainable Garden

GET DIRTY OR GO HOME…BECAUSE SOIL IS THE MOST IMPORTANT PART OF GROWING GOOD FOOD

Plants grow themselves, as long as you supply them with the basics—sunshine, water and soil.

Healthy soil is a living, breathing community composed of microbes, bacteria, fungi, algae, insects, earthworms, minerals, humus and water. Keeping the soil community in top form is the best way to provide nutritious meals for your plants.

Plants and soil organisms have a complex relationship. Even today, scientists do not fully understand how plants and soil organisms interact with each other and the soil to extract nutrients.

Mycorrhizae are tiny soil fungi that grow into the plant roots. Unable to photosynthesize, they extract nitrogen from the environment they share with plants. In turn, plants feed them sugars. A full 80 percent[1] of the world's plants depend on a symbiotic relationship with mycorrhizae to mature. Without plant and fungi symbiosis, many of the foods we love to eat would not exist.

Feed the Soil…Not the Plant

Plants need soil to get a life. Only the best soils produce the crunchiest, juiciest and tastiest vegetables and fruit. Most of the work you do in your garden is to improve and maintain the health of your soil.

There are many types of mycorrhizae and many species of bacteria that help them to form associations with plant roots. As plants mature, their relationship with mycorrhizae changes and they will end one liaison to take up another. Symbiosis between plants and mycorrhizae is fundamental and imperative; attempting to grow plants in soil without the necessary fungi results in weak growth or none at all. Mycorrhizae are harmed by excessive tilling and inorganic and organic pesticides and herbicides.

Nutrient-Rich Humus

Microbes, insects, worms and fungi digest plant and animal wastes—breaking it all down into humus, a rich, fluffy, dark soil full of nutrition. Humus is what you get when decomposition, for the most part, has finished. The food stored in each complex

My Simple Explanation of the Vital Relationship between Plants, Organisms and Soil

Microbes, bacteria, insects, fungi and mycorrhizae are a necessary part of life. They are everywhere—in the forest breaking down last year's leaves and in your garden turning compost into soil. It is impossible and undesirable to eliminate them. Without microbes and fungi we would not be alive.

Mushrooms are the above-ground manifestation of mycorrhizae.

molecule of humus could last forever if not used by plants and microorganisms.

Humus has an astounding ability to absorb water. It shrinks and expands like the elastic waistband on a pair of pants, sucking up water when it rains and drying to dust during a drought. This is why plant cover is so important in keeping soil intact.

Soil Food

Together, plants and microbes break apart the bonds that bind the nutrients to humus. Once the bonds are broken, plants and microbes are free to pick up this nourishment and interact with each other, exchanging nutrients, so plants can grow.

Happy Earthworms

Earthworms mix up the soil by eating organic matter, dragging it down from the surface into their burrows. Air and water flow through the tunnels they create. Plant roots grow into the tunnels, sucking up water and air.

Earthworm wastes (called casts) and microbe excretions contribute to the overall nutrient-richness of humus.

Working Hard

All this work by soil organisms produces carbon dioxide. Plants use the carbon dioxide for photosynthesis, a process that in turn releases the oxygen soil organisms require for decomposition.

These mutually beneficial relationships between plants and soil organisms are fundamental—vital, actually—for a sustainable garden. Disturbances such as pesticides, herbicides, chemical fertilizers, tilling and digging upset this connection and have a corresponding detrimental effect on soil and plant health.

The Trouble with Conventional Vegetable Farms and Gardens

"The trouble with normal is it always gets worse."—Bruce Cockburn

Ordinary mainstream gardens with long rows of carrots and beans—where the soil is constantly being disturbed or drenched with herbicide to eliminate weeds, and where plants are sprayed to get rid of insects—have lost their relationship with the

In a sustainable garden, digging is minimized and herbicides and pesticides are banned—the relationship between soil, plants and soil organisms is protected.

soil. That fundamental rapport between plants, soil organisms and the earth has been destroyed.

If nature's efforts to re-establish the relationship are constantly thwarted, plants and organisms are unable to get the nutrition out of the soil. Soil organisms die and conventional farmers and gardeners are forced to resort to chemical fertilizers to feed the plants.

Why It's Important to Stop Using Inorganic and Organic Pesticides

Nature is a complex web of interconnecting systems. When one part of the web becomes unbalanced, nature works to rebalance itself.

Keeping your plants healthy by keeping the soil alive is the best way to help them resist bug infestations.

By the time we notice an insect invasion, nature is already working on fixing it. A common infestation in gardens and greenhouses is aphids. Given a chance, aphid-eaters, including ladybugs and parasitic wasps, will arrive for this fabulous feast.

Interfering by spraying chemicals—even if they are called "environmentally friendly" or "organic"—kills both bad bugs and the good bugs that have arrived to fight them off. Physical methods of preventing or slowing down bug problems—as in picking or washing insects from your plants—are a better way to deal with the problem while you wait for nature's natural helpers to turn up.

Concerns about the effects of pesticides and herbicides on human health have prompted the Canadian Government to limit their availability. Many pesticides for cosmetic use have been removed from store shelves. All pesticides are regulated through the Pest Control Products Act (PCPA).

The Bare Facts on Why We Shouldn't Use Herbicides

When you spray herbicides to get rid of weeds, you kill all the plant life, exposing bare soil. Mother Nature hates naked ground, as it is so easily blown or washed away and scorched by the sun, upsetting its organisms. She solves the problem by colonizing unprotected earth with what we call invasive weeds—fast-growing, hardy perennials that do a great job of spreading their roots, broadcasting seeds and covering up the soil.

Invasive weeds are nature's first line of defence, rapidly covering bare earth so that a community of soil organisms can re-establish themselves. Think about this the next time you are sweating as you try to yank out hawkweed or oxeye daisy from the once-bare strips of soil between your carefully planted rows of spinach. For more on controlling weeds, see Weeds, a.k.a. Wrong Plant in the Wrong Place, page 76, and Mulch Muchly, page 33.

Minimize Tilling and Digging

Not so long ago, double digging and tilling were *de rigueur*. The best gardens depended on such practices, thought necessary to help plants achieve optimum growth.

Old-school notions like these are so yesterday. We know now that tilling and digging disturbs the community that soil organisms and plant roots have established.

My first garden was built on clay soil. The ancient tiller that came with the place was rusted and falling apart, so I was not surprised when it soon stopped working. Buying a replacement was not in my budget, but digging yards of compost and rotted animal manure into clay was a daunting, exhausting alternative. Meanwhile, my reading insisted that digging amendments into the soil is an unnecessary, pointless waste of effort. Instead, piling manure and compost on top of the soil and then planting encourages worms, insects and microbes to mix up the soil for you. They do this by moving through it, excreting wastes, digesting organic matter, interacting with plant roots and exchanging nutrients.

The presence of mycorrhizae—that extensive network of underground fungi without which most of our plants would cease to exist—is another reason to minimize digging in your garden. Excessive churning and tilling of your soil destroys the mycorrhizae network.

In northern locations, it works wonderfully to pile compost and rotted manure on your gardens in late fall, before the snow flies. By the time the snow has melted in late April or early May, winter's natural freezing and thawing will have broken it down into nice friable soil. As the snowpack thaws and the ground unfreezes, the trickling snowmelt creates channels in the soil for air, water, plant roots and your spade. As soon as the soil dries out, you can start planting the hardiest crops.

Garden Soil 101

The best way to learn something is to just *do it*, making lots of mistakes so that you come to understand the process or concept. If my only focus had been on gardening (and I hadn't been somewhat distracted by raising a family and looking after sheep too), I may have understood earlier that soil is the most important part of the garden. It took working in all of my gardens to learn how to achieve the perfect northern garden.

GARDEN NUMBER ONE: Heavy, Wet, Slimy, Cold Clay Soil

Years before I arrived to take on the post as head gardener in my first vegetable plot, the clay soil—so typical of northern locations (see The Dirt on Soil, page 25)—was being fertilized and improved by the previous gardener, with substantial applications of manure and compost. By the time I got there, it was a deep friable loam. All I had to do to grow an outstanding vegetable garden was sow seeds and occasionally supply the plants with extra water.

Buoyed with success, I dug the turf from a large area of lawn and planted a garden with flowers, shrubs, trees and perennial food plants. I fertilized it with rotted manure from cattle-farming neighbours. Still, every spring, part of this new garden was underwater.

Northern spring—the time when the snow melts and the ground unfreezes—can take as long as two whole months. Slowly thawing ground and impenetrable clay encouraged the melting snow to pool around the plants, killing many of them. The plants that survived grew slowly or not at all. Next, in this same area, I built a raised bed to grow flowers, filling it with chopped-up clay, compost and rotted manure. The herbaceous perennials and bulbs I planted this way grew much better.

Clay soil is wet, heavy and slimy, or dry and hard like concrete. A spade is only useful in spring when defrosted, soggy soil is soft enough to allow you to get one into it. By July, clay soil becomes so unyielding that a pickaxe may not penetrate it. With young children, a sheep farm, and an electric fence to build to keep sheep safe from predators, I didn't have time then to stop to think about why the plants in different areas of the garden grew at different rates or why some of them died. Now, I understand that planting in lighter, fluffier soil in a raised bed erected on top of clay soil is a good strategy, allowing the plants to get growing while organisms in the lighter soil work their way down into the clay below.

GARDEN NUMBER TWO: Light, Gritty, Dry Sandy Soil

I built my second vegetable garden around my house in Prince George. The soil was sandy, and I enriched it by piling compost and manure on top of the beds. Despite my feeling that I constantly needed to water the garden, the plants grew fast—much faster than those in my first garden—and, as a bonus, in the spring there were no pools of water around them.

Because I was still not paying attention to the effect that soil has on plant growth, I thought the plants grew better in this garden because it was a whole two zones warmer than my first property. It wasn't until years later—when my Master Gardener instructor pointed out that the relatively small, sticky particles of clay soil are harder for plants to grow in than coarser, bigger particles of sandy soil—that I began to understand why the plants in this garden grew better than those in my first.

GARDEN NUMBER THREE: Back to Clay Soil

To make the site level for building our third house and garden, the land was heavily bulldozed, a process that removed what little topsoil there was and left behind hard, unyielding clay that even Mother Nature is finding difficult to replant.

Remembering my first clay garden, I piled sandy loam in long rows on top of the clay to plant my annual vegetables in, regularly top dressing with compost and rotted manure. The plants grew well. To stop the soil from washing into the pathways, I erected raised beds, made from untreated 2×10 lumber, in the same areas.

I planted perennials directly into the clay soil, piling soil amendments around them, but soon realized that if I wanted plants like rhubarb to grow faster, I needed to change the soil. I had the choice of digging up the rhubarb crown to replant it in the lighter soil of a raised bed, or I could make a garden bed using an exciting new method called sheet mulching (see What is Sheet Mulching? on page 33).

I'm learning with this third garden that providing the right ingredients is only the first step. Step two is planting the soil with vegetables. And step three is waiting for the soil organisms and plant roots to establish a relationship. In a garden composed of annual plants that die every year, the connections between plants and soil organisms continually need to be renewed.

The Dirt on Soil

Where I live, in northern British Columbia, the soil is relatively young. Ten thousand years ago, glaciers scraped off the topsoil, leaving behind uneven areas of dense clay or sandy gravel. There is very little organic matter. If you want to grow more than native plants or the hardiest of their domestic cousins, you will need to improve your soil.

Clay Soil

Add water to clay and it gets sticky and slimy; take water away and it becomes hard like concrete. While the good news is that clay soil's particles are tiny and hold onto nutrients better than sandy soil, it takes longer to dry out and plants have a harder time putting down roots, so they grow slowly.

Sandy Soil

Add water to sandy soil and it drains quickly through the relatively huge particles. This means plants dry out faster too and soil nutrients leach away more readily. But, looking at the positive side of sandy soil, plants have an easier time putting down roots and grow faster.

The Ultimate Garden Soil

Perfect garden soil retains the best attributes of both clay and sandy soil. The space between particles is small enough that it retains water but not so much that it puddles around plant roots. The resulting soil is light and fluffy, so plants can easily push down roots. The spaces between particles retain enough oxygen to enable soil microbes to breathe, release nutrients and interact with plant roots.

Achieving the Ultimate Garden Soil

Perfect garden soil is like moist chocolate cake, looking dark in colour, feeling light and crumbly yet clumping together when squeezed in your hand. "Loam" and "humus" are words used to describe the best garden soil.

Whether you have sand or clay, or something in-between, the way to make perfect soil remains the same: Add liberal applications of compost and well-rotted manure to provide nutrients as well as improve the soil's texture.

There is no limit to the amount of rotted manure or compost you can add to your garden—the more the better. Nutrients in compost and well-rotted manure are released slowly throughout the growing season, available all the time so plants can take what they need when they need it.

Improving soil texture, encouraging soil organisms, and growing plants is a full-time job for the garden. You can help it work to maximum efficiency with yearly applications of compost and rotted manure.

The Clay-Pot Effect

It wasn't until I took the Master Gardener course that I understood the "clay-pot effect." When you dig a hole in clay soil, fill it with tasty plant nutrients (like compost, rotted manure and bone meal) and then plant something, the surrounding clay acts like a container that fills up with water, drowning the plant. Suddenly I understood why so many of my newly planted trees and shrubs in my first clay garden died.

Send Your Plants Out Into the Real World…Or Why You Should Cut the Apron Strings Early

Even though sandy soil does not suffer from the clay-pot effect, filling holes you've dug for shrubs and trees with nutrients before planting is another quaint, old-school practice like using chalk to write on a slate.

Surrounding new plant roots with nutrients gives them a false start. As soon as their roots grow beyond the treats you have assembled for them, they have to re-adjust to new, not-so-cushy soil conditions.

Get your plants used to real life immediately. Place them directly into your garden soil, piling the soil amendments on top to let the soil organisms do the work for you.

What Do Plants Eat?

Pull out all the stops to preserve the relationship between your soil organisms and plant roots by piling on organic nourishment, keeping the mycorrhizae intact so your garden soil will be the envy of the neighbourhood. Your plants will be stronger, healthier and more productive, easily surpassing those in other gardens to win first prize.

Key Plant Nutrients

Plants get these nutrients ultimately from soil nourished annually with compost and well-rotted manure:

Nitrogen (N): Plants use nitrogen to make chlorophyll, used for photosynthesis, and it keeps them producing green leaves and stems.

Phosphorus (P): Phosphorus helps with root formation.

Potassium (K): Potassium builds proteins that help with photosynthesis, fruit quality and reduction of disease.

Other Nutrients: Calcium, boron, magnesium and iron, among other nutrients, are also required in lesser amounts to help plants grow to their potential.

Slow Food

Slow food is "real" food for plants:

Compost: A good all-round mild fertilizer for every plant, compost contains varying amounts of most nutrients, depending on what substances were used to make it. Plants will happily take as much compost as you can give them. Find out more under Yes, You *Can* Compost in a Cold Climate, page 30.

Rotted Manure: Before being added to your garden, manure needs to be old or well composted, meaning the pile should be turned so that it heats up like compost, destroying weed seeds—see Is It Cooked Yet?, page 29. The fresher the manure is, the faster it will be decomposing—and as it decomposes it produces heat. Good news is that this heat kills weed seeds, however if it is put on your garden at this stage, it will also kill your vegetable seeds and burn plant stems. While old or composted manure unfortunately contains fewer nutrients than relatively fresh manure, its benefits—no weed seeds and a benign nature—make it an excellent soil conditioner and source of nitrogen.

Other Nitrogen Pick-Me-Ups: Coffee grounds, worm castings and blood meal are other good sources of nitrogen.

Calcium: To boost the calcium in your soil, add eggshells, limestone and milk that has gone off (you may as well pour it into the garden—add it to your watering can and irrigate your tomatoes with it to reduce the chances of a condition called blossom end rot; see Blossom End Rot, page 75).

Compost or Manure Tea: Make this to give your plants a healthy boost when you water them. Soak several scoops of compost or rotted manure in a bucket of water until it turns brown. Water your plants with the "tea" when the soil surrounding them is dry. Feed as much to your plants as you want—it will not burn their roots like too much chemical fertilizer does.

Fast Food

Plant fast food comes in bottles or bags. It has numbers corresponding to the amount of major plant nutrients (NPK) they contain. Like human fast food, it goes down great but its consequences are harmful.

Fast-food fertilizers feed the plant, not the soil. Plants can only use chemical fertilizer when they are growing. If they are dormant, the fertilizer is wasted and washes away, contaminating water sources.

Plants fed too much chemical fertilizer look like they are on steroids. They are freakishly bigger than their normal-sized cousins who are fed sensible diets of compost and well-rotted manure.

Fixating on Nitrogen Fixation

Legumes, plants from the Fabaceae or Leguminosae family, get nitrogen through a process called nitrogen fixation. They extract nitrogen from the air, and with the aid of specialized *Rhizobium* bacteria, convert it into amino acids that are deposited into nodules on their roots.

Common legumes grown in gardens and on farms or found in the wilds in the north include peas (*Pisum sativum*), beans (*Phaseolus*), fava beans (*Vicia faba*), lupines (*Lupinus*), sweet peas (*Lathyrus odoratus*), clover (*Trifolium*), sweet clover (*Melilotus albus*), alfalfa (*Medicago sativa*) and Siberian peashrub (*Caragana*). Each legume species needs a different *Rhizobium* species to fix nitrogen. If the specific bacteria required are not in the soil, nitrogen fixation will not occur.

Garden centres sell Rhizobium bacteria to inoculate beans and peas before planting them. To inoculate legumes, mix together a tablespoon of water, seeds and enough inoculate to coat them. Add a teaspoon of sugar to help the inoculate stick to the seeds. Plant seeds immediately for maximum effect.

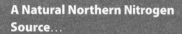

A Natural Northern Nitrogen Source...

There are several species of Alnus viridis (alder) native to the northern hemisphere. I have natural hedges of these shrubs growing at the edges of my garden. The Alnus genus belongs to the Betulaceae family, but unlike the other genera in this family, it is capable of nitrogen fixation.

Mushrooms Are Good

Although scientists do not yet understand how they do it, fungi are capable of fixing nitrogen just like legumes.

In her acclaimed book *Eating Dirt*, author Charlotte Gill says mushrooms are the above-ground fruit of a vast fungi network. The network, called mycorrhizae, has a symbiotic relationship with plants. Fungi exchange the nitrogen they fix for the plants' sugars. Without mushrooms and the underground mycorrhizae, many of our edible plants would not exist. Much of the food we eat depends on a symbiotic relationship with mycorrhizae to grow, flower and fruit.

When I see mushrooms growing in my garden, I leave them alone or at the very least add them to my compost. Plants that make their own nitrogen should be highly valued.

How to Grow Nitrogen for Your Soil

Plants use nitrogen to grow bigger and stronger. Some northern farmers plant fields of peas specifically to take advantage of their nitrogen-fixing abilities. At the end of the summer, they turn the plants back into the soil, letting them rot. This process is called green manuring.

Mushrooms are capable of fixing nitrogen to fertilize the soil and thus feed the plants.

You can do the same thing in your garden: grow a green-manure crop to cover the soil and fertilize it at the same time. Choose any of the legume plants listed in Fixating on Nitrogen Fixation, page 27. Even a small crop of peas or beans benefits your soil. Once you have harvested them, simply leave the plants and roots in the garden to decompose, releasing nitrogen into the soil for next year's crop.

The Best Ways to Get Manure Don't Stink

Raising animals is the ideal way to acquire rotted manure. Manure from rabbits, chickens, goats, sheep, horses, llamas, pigs and cows is all good.

The next best place to get manure is to ask a farmer, horsey friend or someone raising chickens in their backyard if you can have their manure. Farm markets are great places to meet farmers. Advertising for manure on Craigslist, Kijiji or The Freecycle

Well-rotted manure is an ideal plant food and great soil conditioner. Every year, I pushed all the manure from the barnyard onto this pile; what I didn't use I gave away to enlightened gardeners.

Network is easy and rewarding. The people who hang out on these message boards are generally friendly and more than willing to let you have the stuff they no longer have use for.

Is It Cooked Yet?

Unlike compost, manure is better when it has been cured. Fresh manure is full of weed seeds that will sprout in your garden, increasing your workload and driving you crazy. And there is a small risk contaminates that would adversely affect your crops or your health may be present in fresh manure. Besides the weed seeds and health worries, fresh manure also emits heat as it decomposes, and this heat could burn your plants.

Old rotted manure is a mild substance containing no weed seeds—it's a perfect food for your soil. The amount of time manure needs to sit before it is ready for your garden depends on how the farmer has treated it. If the farmer is actively turning a huge pile of manure, it will heat up and decompose faster; this manure should be ready for use in a few months. If the manure has been piled into a corner and left to sit, it could take a few years before it is ready for your garden.

What's a Hot Bed?

As manure decomposes, it produces heat. Traditional hot beds make use of this heat to start plants earlier in the season. The decomposing manure keeps seedlings warm and supplies them with extra carbon dioxide, enhancing growth. With careful planning and monitoring, a hot bed could be used as a sustainable way to get your tender seedlings outside earlier.

Bringing Home Animal Poo

Sometimes farmers clean out their pens and paddocks, piling the manure in an unused corner, where it is usually forgotten. Where this is the case, get the manure from the oldest pile—it will be the most rotted down and have the best chance of containing no weed seeds or other undesirable elements. Don't worry if there are weeds growing on top of it. Weeds are opportunists and old manure piles are light and crumbly and a great source of nutrition.

All you need is a container and a shovel. Sometimes, if you have a pickup truck, the farmer may load it for you. Most times you will have to shovel it yourself.

Compost and manure are rich in soil organisms, forming an active relationship with plant roots. Nutrients are easily shared and plants grow bigger and stronger.

Yes, You *Can* Compost in a Cold Climate

Compost is a free, organic, non-toxic source of nutrition for your plants. It's easy to make—throw everything into a pile in a sunny spot, then simply let it sit around until it turns to soil. Let insects, microbes, worms, ants, rain and the sun do the work for you.

Compost Fixings

Every garden needs a compost heap—and it is the ideal place to throw all your organic wastes:

- Leaves
- Vegetable peelings
- Eggshells
- Plant trimmings
- Contents of your vacuum bag
- Hair from your brush
- Coffee grounds
- Tea leaves
- Stale bread
- Paper
- Dryer lint
- Banana skins
- Rotting food from the bottom of your fridge
- Crustacean shells
- Grass clippings (chemical free)
- Garden weeds (see sidebar)

The more nitrogen you add to your pile, the faster it will decompose. Good sources of nitrogen include coffee grounds (ask your coffee shop for their used grounds), tea leaves, livestock manures and human urine (some people swear that peeing in their compost improves its nutritional content).

At the end of the season, pile your garden waste into compost bins, layering it with kitchen scraps, coffee grounds and other organic materials.

Weeds Your Compost Needs

When adding weeds to your compost pile, ensure there are no seed heads. Most weeds are extremely hardy and chances are their seeds will not be killed by the heat in your home compost. Send the seedy parts of weeds to the municipal landfill for composting there (see More Compost, page 33) and add the rest of the plants to your pile.

Seedless weeds with long taproots—like Taraxacum officinale *(dandelion)—are fabulous for your compost heap because they bring up minerals from deep within the ground.*

Symphytum officinale (comfrey) is a hardy perennial herb that is great at mining the soil for nutrients. It contains phosphorus, potassium, magnesium and more. Grow it in your garden, let it compost in place or cut it back to use the leaves as mulch or compost.

Make Compost Before the Snow Flies

The best time to assemble a compost pile or put down sheet mulch (see What is Sheet Mulching?, page 33) is in fall before the ground freezes and snow arrives, usually around the end of October. During the winter, the compost eventually freezes solid, but all the thawing and refreezing it does at the beginning and end of winter breaks it down. By the time the snow melts and you can get your spade into the pile, most of the work is done.

Traditionally, compost heaps are layered, with close attention paid to the carbon-to-nitrogen ratio (which apparently should be 30 parts carbon to 1 part nitrogen, although I never worry about this). The stuff is turned regularly to help it heat up and speed up the process of decomposition. As the organic matter decays, nutrients are released. Compost is "done" when it has turned into a fine crumbly soil. But, by this time, many of its mineralized nutrients have washed away.

Adding partially decomposed compost to your garden increases soil-organism activity and the availability of nutrients for your plants. Of course, you may get the odd beet top or tomato seed sprouting...don't worry, just pull it up and send it back to the compost heap.

There is recent research[2] to suggest that all this aggressive turning of the compost pile speeds up decomposition to the point that many of the nutrients are leached away before they even get to your garden. Letting the pile sit in the sun without turning it slows decomposition and mineral loss.

In my garden, I let the compost heap decompose into soil by itself.

At the end of the season, after harvesting, I leave the leaves and stems of herbaceous perennials—like comfrey, horseradish, asparagus and chives—to decompose in the garden. I let the remaining leaves from harvested annuals, such as lettuce, beans, peas and cauliflower, stay in the garden to decompose as well. Come spring most of it is gone, save for a few tough stalks that I pull up and throw on the compost pile.

Of course, if I'm making a new garden, the dying plants are an excellent ingredient (again, see What is Sheet Mulching?, page 33).

Keep It Close When It's Cold

My compost heap is far away from the house, behind the greenhouse. As winter is most often a seven-month snowy, sub-zero sojourn, it is easier for me to stockpile my compost ingredients every winter in a black plastic composter by my back door.

The composter is a bottomless black plastic shell with a lid. It's anchored to the ground with plastic screws. The lid keeps out snow. Without a lid, it would fill up with snow so quickly there would be no room for compost material. It's easy and quick to dash outside, brush off the snow, lift up the lid and tip in my bucket of kitchen scraps.

When winter is over, I remove the screws, lift the plastic shell off the accumulated pile and transfer all this partially rotted stuff over to the main compost heap.

My primary composter has two bins made from logs, leftover chicken wire and plywood. It has no lid and regularly gets rained on. During a prolonged summer drought, it is easy enough to water the compost with the hose when I'm already over there watering the tomatoes in the greenhouse—keeping compost moist helps it to break down. In winter, the whole thing freezes solid and is deeply covered in snow…and I forget all about it.

I keep this plastic compost bin next to my back door all winter, where it is handy to fill.

When to Put Compost on the Garden

I put my partially decomposed compost on the gardens in the spring after the annual plants have germinated and are actively growing. The soil organisms quickly work on it, releasing nutrients that are happily taken up by the plants.

In the fall, after the vegetables have finished growing, I spread compost on top of the beds for next year or leave most of the plant remains in the beds to decompose in situ.

October is a good time to spread compost around the trunks of shrubs and trees and crowns of herbaceous plants, when they are semi-dormant and before the snow falls—come spring, when the plants wake up and start growing, they can take advantage of the nutrients. I never worry about how much compost I'm spreading around my perennials. Unlike chemicals, too much compost will not burn the plants' roots. The amount I use is simply limited to how much I have—and there never seems to be enough.

More Compost

Municipal landfills are a great source of huge amounts of reasonably priced compost. These places make super-sized compost piles that are bigger than your house. Compost from a landfill is regularly turned and heated to a very high temperature, killing not only weed seeds but annihilating and rendering inert lawn chemicals, pesticides and herbicides. It is tested and deemed safe for your garden. You can buy it by the yard—a bucketful from a front-end loader—and will need a pickup truck to take it away; it's worth borrowing or even renting one, as this is the cheapest source of compost available (outside of making it yourself).

What is Sheet Mulching?

Better and easier than tilling or actively turning a compost heap, sheet mulching is a way of incorporating organic waste into the garden, a means of making soil directly in the bed. Simply pile up your organic matter, top it with a layer of finished compost and then tuck in your plants or seedlings.

Make a Sheet-Mulched Garden Bed

I use sheet mulching to make new garden beds directly on top of my lawn. The first layer is cardboard or several thicknesses of newspaper to suppress weeds. As you lay it down, spray it with water to keep the paper or cardboard from blowing away and to help it rot faster. On top of the cardboard or paper, pile a mixture of as much organic matter as you have: grass clippings, kitchen scraps, compost, rotted manure, straw and/or wood chips. If you are using lots of high-carbon material—like wood chips, straw and sawdust—sprinkle on extra nitrogen in the form of manure, coffee grounds or blood meal to help balance out the carbon–nitrogen ratio.

Sheet mulching is not an exact science: the types of materials you lay down and amount of each can reflect what you have available. Use weed-free finished compost or well-rotted manure for the top layer.

Sheet mulch a new garden in late fall before the snow flies. Plant perennials directly in the top layer of finished compost or rotted manure. By the time spring arrives months later, the soil organisms will be in top form, interacting with the newly growing roots of your perennials to digest the organic matter laid down in the sheet mulch. Your plants will respond by luxuriously spreading their roots into the new deep organic matter and putting out lots of healthy new top growth.

Spring is the time to plant seeds in your new sheet-mulched bed. They'll grow fast, swiftly putting down roots and lapping up all that delicious organic nourishment.

Mulch Muchly

You can use almost anything to mulch your plants. The type of mulch you pick depends on what purpose it will have, and what you have available.

Mulch is used to keep weeds away, warm up the soil, cool down the soil, keep the soil moist, keep plants frozen, keep plants warm, encourage soil activity and increase available nutrients.

Apart from encouraging soil-organism activity and increasing nutrient availability, finished compost and well-rotted manure are used as a mulch to prevent weeds from germinating—lay down a good inch (2.5 cm) over the entire garden.

For more on mulching, see Use Mulch to Retain Moisture, page 70, and Use Mulch to Keep Plants Frozen All Winter, page 44.

What to Do With Fallen Leaves

I wait until spring to rake up the dead leaves from the driveway and parking area to add them to the compost bins. I leave dead leaves and plant remains where they have fallen within the gardens. In spring, as the land thaws, the perennials start to grow, and the soil organisms wake up and get to work on decomposing the dead plants and leaves, releasing nutrients. This way, the soil is not disturbed and the relationship between the plants and soil organisms is maintained.

The Sincerest Form of Flattery

I mimic nature by letting the stalks and leaves of perennials like rhubarb, sorrel, comfrey and asparagus die back naturally. The dead stuff acts like mulch, helping to keep the crowns of these plants firmly rooted in the earth—this way, the thawing and freezing cycles at the beginning and end of winter won't heave them out of the ground where their exposed roots will be killed. In the spring, I leave the dead stuff in the garden to fertilize new growth. I do the same with the leaves that fall off woody perennials.

Letting leaves lie where they fall returns nutrients to the soil and helps keep plant crowns frozen and safely tucked in all winter.

Garden Self-Sustainability

In the beginning—when you are first establishing your gardens, creating beds and planting perennials—you'll need to add enormous amounts of rotted manure and compost. As your fruit trees, shrubs, vines and herbaceous perennials grow and fill out, the garden will start to look after itself.

The garden will recycle its own wastes—fallen leaves, dying perennial tops, pulled weeds and annual plants— into food. The need for you to make annual trips for truckloads of manure or compost will be over.

Planting close together and covering bare soil in the annual vegetable beds with compost not only feeds the plants but also slows down evaporation, keeping the amount of watering you have to do to a minimum. See Quench Plant Thirst, page 69, for more on watering plants.

Soon, the only work you will need to do is to plant seeds, nurture seedlings and harvest food.

Invest Now for the Future

It takes considerable time to produce quality, friable garden soil. I didn't really understand this until I started building my third garden. Bringing home manure and municipal compost, sheet mulching, making a compost pile and composting in situ in the garden are all investments in the future.

Dead rhubarb stems and leaves return nutrients to the soil for next year's crop.

Quality soil encourages robust soil communities, a place where organisms and plant roots develop strong, vigorous, thriving relationships.

Happy soil communities are dynamic—they produce healthy plants that live longer and are better able to resist disease, drought, insect infestations, temperature swings, hail, floods and strong winds.

Produce from sustainably grown plants tastes better, contains no potentially harmful substances, has a longer shelf life and gives you peace of mind.

CHAPTER 2

Maximize Your Results

THE COLD-CLIMATE FOOD GARDEN IS ALL ABOUT MAKING THE MOST OF WHAT LITTLE HEAT CAN BE GATHERED FROM THE SUN

Pick the sunniest place for your vegetable garden. Except for one week in July and even then only during the hottest part of the day, your plants will thank you for the sunlight and warmth. And who cares if the sunniest spot in your garden is your front lawn? The neighbours will get used to it and may even copy you. Fast-growing annual vegetables and flowers need as much heat as they can get. Even cool-weather crops and early-spring perennials benefit from extra heat.

In very early spring, late April and May, the frost is still melting out of the ground, and almost every night temperatures plunge below zero Celsius (32F). At this time of

June in the vegetable garden…planted in full sun for maximum plant growth. Raised beds help snow to melt quicker and soil to heat up faster. The clover lawn surrounding the beds provides extra nutrition in the form of nitrogen, due to its innate ability to fix atmospheric nitrogen; plus clover flowers attract pollinating insects.

year, the amount of heat the sun puts out is so feeble it's like trying to warm a house with a candle. By knowing how to increase the temperature around your plants, you can get them growing faster and harvest a crop sooner.

Know Your Microclimates

Get outside and really look at your garden. Do this at different times of the day and varying periods of the year. Do it from the deck, the lawn and the driveway. Look out the windows of your house, and at the garden from the open doorway.

Pay attention to the sun: notice where it is shining and for how long. Does the amount of sunlight depend on the time of day or the season? How does cloud cover affect the sunlight in each part of your garden?

Notice what areas of your garden are sheltered from wind, where the snow melts first, and which spots get frosted earliest in fall. Pay attention to what plants leaf out first in spring. Does the same plant in a different location leaf out later?

Each area of your yard has its own particular microclimate. Those that are warmer are important in northern gardens because they help you to maximize your growing opportunities. Taking advantage of the warmer pockets in your yard may make it possible to grow plants rated for a warmer zone, or to ripen harvests earlier.

Be Enlightened about Light

"I wear my sunglasses at night."–Corey Hart

In winter I wear my sunglasses during the day. If it's not snowing outside, the sun is bouncing its rays off the snow on the ground, increasing their intensity. In the north, winter sunshine is the default weather—it keeps winter bearable and almost makes up for its insane length of seven months.

Yet, despite its abundance, northern sunlight is weak, even in summer. Nature makes up for it by increasing the day length, enabling northern gardeners to grow and ripen food in a shorter time than gardeners farther south. Maximize the sunlight from these longer days by planting your vegetable garden in a location with full sun. My garden in the BC Peace did not have to contend with shadows from buildings or trees, and got the full-day length of sunlight that peaks at the summer solstice in June and then drops off gradually, so that by the middle of August the days are dramatically shortening with a corresponding decline in plant growth.

Some spring vegetables, such as arugula, sorrel, lettuce, cilantro and spinach, may benefit from a little shade in July to slow down their inevitable bolting (going to seed). You can minimize bolting by planting them on the north side of taller plants, like peas, bush beans, pole beans and potatoes. (And snipping plants back just as their seed heads are forming interrupts their natural propensity to bolt.)

Feel the Heat or (More Likely) Lack of Heat

The snow has melted away, and while the temperature may be just above zero, the calendar says June, so the plants grow leaves and flowers. Some northern humans have the same reaction, tending to use the calendar rather than temperature as a guide to when it's time to wear flip-flops and shorts. I never managed to master this devotion to the calendar when it comes to deciding what to wear. Luckily, the plants don't care when I show up in the cold spring garden wearing mitts and two sweaters under my coat.

Spring-blooming plants need less heat than summer-bloomers and go dormant in July and early August…but by late August, when it's relatively cool, they start growing again.

Take Shelter

Warm-weather crops, like tomatoes and peppers, need full sunlight and lots of heat. Plant them in a sheltered area, such as against a wall on the south side of a building. The wall absorbs the sun's heat, radiating it back at the nearby plants, keeping them snug. And the snow melts away from these areas first. Plant early-harvest perennial vegetables, like sorrel, rhubarb and asparagus, in protected microclimates to enjoy the tastes of spring earlier.

Know Your Snow

Snow melts first on south-facing slopes. Building your annual vegetable garden on a subtle south-facing slope means snow disappears faster, exposed soil heats up and dries out earlier, and you can plant your seeds sooner.

Snow cover protects the roots of perennials by keeping them frozen and dormant: normal freezing and thawing cycles at the beginning and end of the season may force plant crowns out of the ground, killing the exposed roots. Prevent this by leaving dead stems and leaves of herbaceous perennials intact to hold on to the snow. This is especially valuable where snow cover is scanty or most of the snowpack has melted before winter is over.

Face Off Frost

Frost slides down slopes, gathers in low spots and is always denser on the north side of buildings and north-facing slopes.

Plant crops that taste better after frost, such as Brussels sprouts or rutabagas, at the bottom of your slightly south-sloping vegetable garden. When the first frosts arrive in late summer in zone 2 and early fall in zone 3, they may simply skim across the garden, burning only the tips of plants.

Warm-weather crops, on the other hand, are the most susceptible to frost damage, and need to be protected by a tarp, row cover or piece of plastic (see Crop Covers, page 39).

Use Wind Power

The BC Peace—home of my first garden—is windy; in fact, I got so used to the wind that when I moved to Prince George, I missed it. In the north, wind blows away mosquitoes and other biting bugs, definitely a bonus. Not as good, in the winter, gusts and gales blow the light, dry snow about, creating huge unmanageable drifts that are difficult to remove without big machinery.

With careful planning, you may be able to design your garden to use wind power to pile snow on top of your perennials: Try cleverly growing them on the lee side of fences and buildings, or erecting temporary structures to encourage snow to mound. Snow cover keeps plants frozen and safe.

Plant warm-weather crops in sheltered spots to keep them out of the wind. And be sure to harden off the seedlings you've coddled indoors to help them get used to wind before you plant them out (see How to Harden Off Plants, page 66).

Stake tall vegetables, like lovage, sunflowers, dill, peppers and tomatoes, to keep them upright in brisk breezes.

A Good Stake

As long as it is strong enough to support the plant, any stick will make a stake. Garden centres and hardware stores sell stakes made of various materials. I cut down unwanted poplar trees and willows from the bush around my house to use as stakes. I have also made some from leftover rebar and wood from various building projects.

Tie the plant, as it grows, to the stake, using any material. Garden centres sell green Velcro tape specific for staking. I have been known to use lengths of old t-shirts, pantyhose and even masking tape. What's most important is to not wait until the plant falls over—stake it when it is small and continue to add ties as necessary.

Look for Cover—Making Microclimates

In cold climates, employing tactics to keep tender plants warm and protected from harsh winds is especially valuable at the beginning and end of the growing season—giving them a good start and helping them to ripen before they are killed by frost.

Warm-weather crops benefit from extra heat provided by crop covers.

Frost Protection

When frost threatens toward the end of the season and I want to eke out every last bit of growth from warm-weather crops, I cover them overnight with a tarp. Blankets or pieces of plastic or other flexible cloth are also good options. Take the cover off the next day after the sun is high in the sky and frost has melted away.

Covering your plants overnight to keep frost off works great until you forget, go away overnight, or just can't be bothered anymore… besides, you can't keep winter away forever.

Crop Covers

A crop cover is a lightweight, flexible white cloth

that allows water and sunlight to pass through. Available from garden centres, you can adjust its size by cutting it into pieces, or use it full-size to cover large beds or even your whole garden.

Use crop covers to keep heat around warm-weather edibles all season, to help them mature and ripen. In my garden, the plants most in need of a cozy cover are beans, cucumber, summer squash, tomatoes, pepper and basil. Attach a crop cover to a frame and it becomes a cold frame (see below). Or keep things simple, as I do, and just drape the crop cover loosely over the plants, using rocks or other heavy weights on the corners to keep it from blowing away. As the season progresses, you may need to adjust the weights that hold it in place so as not to restrict plant growth.

Take the crop cover off the plants during the day when it is hot, and replace it in the evening before it gets cold, trapping the lingering heat. Sometimes though, during short, cool summers, you may find yourself keeping the cover on the crops all day and night. Crop covers also offer a few degrees of frost protection and help to keep pesky bugs off your plants (see How to Discourage Damaging Insects, page 73).

Cloches

A glass jar placed over a single seedling to keep it warm in early spring, "cloche" means bell and was originally used in the gardens of France. Make a cloche by slicing the bottom off a large plastic pop bottle or milk jug. Sink the cloche firmly into the soil so it doesn't blow away, removing the lid during the day to provide ventilation to the plant inside.

For more on cold frames, crop covers and cloches, see the colour insert after page 64.

In northern gardens, you will only be using cloches for a week or two—it won't be long until the baby seedlings become gangly teenagers too large to be contained.

Cold Frame

Cold frames are rigid structures usually placed over a garden bed. I've seen them made from glass windows or plastic sheeting. If they're lightweight, they can be moved around the garden and used to protect crops from frost and wind in early spring as well as in the fall. It can work well to remove the cold frame during the day and replace it over the plants at night.

I've seen other effective cold frames rigged onto hoops attached to the sides of a raised bed. A row cover is anchored down over the hoops when frost is imminent. When the weather warms up, it is easy to peel back the cover until the next cold spell threatens.

Still other cold frames are permanent structures with lids that are opened or shut depending on the weather.

Greenhouse

My passive solar greenhouse is a free-standing structure that protects my tomatoes and peppers to at least -5C (23F), although the plant parts touching the windows may get frosted. In addition to low temperatures, greenhouses guard plants from hailstorms, wind and other rough weather. Having a greenhouse means I can get my tender plants into it and growing before the last frost date.

Water-filled milk jugs absorb heat, helping to moderate the temperature in my greenhouse, particularly during cool summer nights.

Heat Things Up in the Greenhouse

Water is a better heat conductor than air. Once water has heated up, it cools down slower than air. Take advantage of water's amazing heat-storing capacity, and use water and the heat from the sun to keep plants in your greenhouse warm. This is especially valuable at either end of the season when nighttime frost is expected.

I fill plastic milk jugs with water from the tap or from my rain barrels and place them around the tomato plants in the greenhouse. During the day, the water absorbs the sun's heat, getting hotter. At night, the heat from the water radiates out, keeping my plants warm.

The bigger the store of water, the more warmth it will absorb and the longer it takes to cool down. This is an easy and inexpensive way to retain heat in an enclosed space like a greenhouse or cold frame.

I get my greenhouse ready for planting sometime in early May, depending on the weather and how fast the snow is melting. The first task is soil rehydration. During the long seven-month winter, the ground outside and soil inside the greenhouse are frozen. In spring, the soil outside is soaked with melting snow as it thaws. As there is no melting snow inside the greenhouse, I have to rehydrate the soil myself with water from the tap. It takes a couple of hours. If I could lift the roof off the greenhouse for winter, I wouldn't have to do this.

Next, I plant the seedlings and surround each of them with compost to give them a nutritional boost to help them get established in their new home.

After the greenhouse is planted, I regularly check on growth, staking and watering the plants. By mid-July, soaring daytime temperatures make the greenhouse

In midsummer I leave the greenhouse door open to help regulate the heat.

excessively hot, so I open the window at the back and the door at the front to allow a cross breeze to cool the greenhouse and evaporate excess humidity. I close them at night.

It's always a conundrum when I go on a summer holiday as to whether I should leave the greenhouse door open or keep it shut. I learned the hard way that too much heat kills tomato flowers. Dead flowers equal no fruit.

Since then, a friend has shown me the window-opening mechanism, sensitive to heat, that she has attached to the windows in her greenhouse. Another friend has set up a self-watering system for her greenhouse, with sensors to detect moisture around the plant roots. Outside containers, which collect water from the greenhouse roof, are fitted with pipes to carry the water to individual plants when the sensors detect soil dryness. With her greenhouse set up like this, she's free to head off for an extended summer sojourn.

Sunlight Kills Mould

There is lots of literature about the importance of keeping a greenhouse scrupulously clean to avoid disease and bugs that may overwinter in it. I confess I'm lazy: I've never washed my greenhouse or plant pots. I even leave potting soil in clay pots stored inside the house so the pots don't freeze, crack and break. I haven't had any problems.

Sunlight kills mould: I've used it to sterilize children's diapers, cutting boards and the compost pail. I'm sure that plenty of northern sunlight combined with ridiculously long, sub-zero, insect-killing winters have helped me stay on the right side of disease and bug control.

Rocks for Heat

Some of my early-spring perennials—asparagus, sorrel and chives—are planted in a garden bed backed by rock walls. The rocks absorb the sun's heat, radiating it back out to the plants. Before the snow has entirely melted from other parts of the garden, these edibles are up and growing, giving me an early harvest. By mid-July, these plants are too hot and going to seed and dying back. But it doesn't matter, as the asparagus is over by then anyway and I have chives and sorrel planted in cooler parts of the garden for later harvests.

Heat-loving oregano revels in the extra heat radiating off the rocks in this garden bed; the chives also benefit from this warmth by winning the prize for the first clump in my garden to sprout and grow in spring.

Warm-weather crops planted in front of rocks eagerly soak up the extra heat. Thyme, oregano, sage, squash, beans, tomatoes, peppers and other heat lovers enjoy this warmth throughout their growing season.

Raised Beds

Raising your beds is a way to warm the soil earlier. In northern gardens, anything you can do to melt the snow, dry out the soil and warm it up faster helps you plant the garden earlier—and enjoy harvests sooner.

Raised beds also get the plants off any inhospitable clay soil (see Clay Soil, page 25) and improve drainage, so they grow better. The plants you grow for food prefer lighter soil that is easy for them to get their roots into (see The Ultimate Garden Soil, page 25).

Raise Soil Up to Warm It Up

Making a raised bed may be as simple as mounding up the soil into berms and planting on top of it. I did this with my vegetable garden in the BC Peace: I divided my garden plot, building it into long rows of mounded soil about 25–30 cm (10-12 in) high and about 20–30 cm (8–12 in) wide. The space between the mounds was just a few inches—barely enough for me to walk along.

In my current garden, I built beds out of untreated 2×10 lumber and filled them with a mixture of compost, manure and clay, or I laid down sheet mulching (see What is Sheet Mulching?, page 33) to make soil. I built another raised bed using rocks along a south-facing slope—the snow melts here first. It's exciting to see my early-spring bulbs flowering and to be able to harvest sorrel leaves and chives while other parts of the garden are still covered by melting snow.

Use Mulch to Keep Plants Frozen All Winter

In garden zones 2 and 3, the ground freezes as much as 2.4 m (8 ft) deep and stays that way all winter for 6–7 months. It's not the length of time that the ground is frozen that matters but rather the number of times the top few centimetres freeze and thaw and refreeze at the beginning and end of winter. This process can heave the crowns of your plants out of the ground, leaving exposed roots to freeze and die.

Worry About the Beginning and End of Winter…
Plants are at risk of being thrust out of the ground in late fall before a persistent snow cover, and in late spring after most of the snow has melted.

Chinooks—dry, warm winter winds that blow on the east side of the Rocky Mountains and heat up the air temperature to a few degrees above zero Celsius, plunging it back down to -20C (-4F) in as little as 24 hours—have minimal effect on the vast white fields of ice and snow that cover the northern winter landscape. Chinooks are common across the prairies and in the BC Peace where I grew my first garden.

Protect your plants by leaving their own leaves where they fall and the dead stalks of herbaceous perennials intact to trap the first early-winter snow. Additionally, spread leaves, sawdust, bark or straw around the crowns of plants. I've also heard of people laying old boards on top of their plants to keep them frozen and safe. And the very best mulch is a nice deep layer of snow—shovel it onto your garden plants to replace what blows away.

Mulch Makers

As summer turns into fall, plants stop growing and shed their leaves onto the ground, where soil organisms break them down into the humus that supplies food for the garden, keeping soil moist and perpetuating a healthy growing environment.

Plants with big leaves make more mulch. Plant Jerusalem artichoke, rhubarb, potato and stinging nettle. Leave dead stems and leaves of these plants in the garden to decompose or toss them on the compost.

Leaving dead foliage in place traps snow, keeping plants from being heaved out of the ground during late-fall and early-spring freezing and thawing cycles. The fallen leaves rot, returning nutrition to the soil that this lovage plant can benefit from in the new growing season.

Root Busters

Some plants—such as dandelion, chicory, daikon radish, comfrey, mustard, alfalfa and clover—have roots that break up the soil. Plant them as a cover crop or between your crops and around shrubs and trees. As a bonus, their stems and leaves break down into humus and their enormous root systems decay in situ, aerating the soil and increasing nutrition.

You may have noticed that most plants perform more than one role. The more functions a plant fulfills the more valuable it becomes as a citizen in your sustainable garden—see Make the Most of Multiple Plant Features, page 50.

Consider Companion Planting

Pick the right companions or friends and your life becomes more enjoyable and rewarding. The same goes for your plants. Good plant companions help each other out and improve each other's growth potential.

By making use of your yard's microclimates, you can grow as many plants as possible and increase your garden's diversity. Variety is the key to a sustainable garden. Different plants complement each other.

Onions, carrots, dill, lemon balm and shungiku grow happily in the same raised bed.

Confuse Pests

Companion planting is as simple as planting two different crops next to each other. Breaking up your garden rows with herbs and flowers confuses pests—so that instead of going from lettuce to lettuce in a mass planting, hungry bugs may only chew holes in a few of them and not notice the rest.

Avoid Nutrient Competition

Plants have varying root systems that mine the soil at different depths for the same nutrients. To avoid competition, plant deep-rooted carrots, medium-rooted greens and shallow-rooted alliums in the same bed.

Attract Beneficial Insects

Insect-attracting companion plants offer nectar, pollen and foliage for habitat and food. In northern gardens, wild plants like clover, cinquefoil, yarrow and dandelion, along with escaped alfalfa from farmers' fields, do this job for you. Take advantage of nature's beneficial offerings and let some of these plants grow in your garden, perhaps in the paths between raised beds or in the hedgerows along the edges of your yard.

Borage flowers attract bees and other pollinators to your garden—and they're edible too.

Other insect-attracting plants you can cultivate include dill, cilantro, thyme, borage, marigolds and nasturtiums. By growing a variety of plant species, diversity is increased and desirable bugs will outnumber bad bugs. Still, remember that both are necessary to keep a garden community thriving. For example, without aphids and other prey, there would be no parasitic wasps or other predators. It takes all kinds to make the garden a happy home for your plants.

Add Nitrogen

Legumes like peas and beans fix nitrogen from the air, making it available to plants growing next to them (see Fixating on Nitrogen Fixation, page 27). It works well to plant heavy feeders where legume crops have recently grown (and where you have left the roots and maybe some of the plant material to decompose in the ground), to take advantage of the extra nitrogen in the soil. Good candidates for this are plants from the Brassicaceae or Cruciferae family, such as broccoli, cabbage, Brussels sprouts and kale. Hardy herbaceous perennials like clover and alfalfa, shrubs such as Siberian peashrub, and trees like alder and Russian olive are nitrogen fixers and valuable additions to your sustainable garden.

Long-rooted clover brings up water and nutrients from deep within the soil and fixes nitrogen, benefitting the shallow-rooted Swiss chard and onions. Also, the scent of the onions discourages plant-eating insects from the chard.

Add Minerals

Deep-rooted plants are classic mineral collectors that concentrate calcium, magnesium, sulphur and potassium in their leaves. When the leaves die, the minerals are released into the soil. In northern gardens, such plants include lamb's quarters, plantain, chives, chicory, dandelion, Egyptian onion, fennel, garlic, stinging nettle and watercress.

What to Grow Where

Choose planting spots according to how plants grow:

Perennials and Biennials

Plant your perennials and biennials in the ground where their roots stay nice and safe, covered deeply by soil, mulch and—if you are lucky—snow. Planting permanent plants in pots means they will die when their roots freeze, unfreeze and freeze again. I've seen zealots go to extreme lengths with Styrofoam and other insulators to keep potted perennials alive. I say forget it. Plant your hardy perennials and biennials directly in the ground and stop worrying about them.

Annuals

If any plants are designed to grow in pots, it's annuals. In northern gardens, this also means tender perennials, which wither and die at the first whisper of frost, and are often grown as annuals. Their shallow root systems take up little room, and it's easy to move their pots around to accommodate the plants' exacting requirements: lots of heat, abundant water and constant deadheading. Keeping them close to the house during their summer outdoor sojourn makes it easier to remember to cover them overnight or bring them inside if frost threatens.

Tips for Growing Annuals in Pots:

- Remember to check pots more or less daily—depending on the weather—for dryness, and water them accordingly. Plants grown in pots dry out faster than those in the garden.
- Unless you're having problems with insects, there is no need to put fresh soil in a pot every year. I've had the same soil in my pots for six years.
- Boost nutrition in your pots with a top dressing of finished compost every spring. Or water the pots with compost or manure tea (see Compost or Manure Tea, page 27).

Choosing Plant Containers:

- You can grow plants in any container—just remember to punch holes in the bottom for drainage.
- Big containers need less watering than small containers, which dry out quickly.
- Plastic containers retain moisture better than clay pots and need less watering.
- Clay pots are prettier and they breathe, but they dry out faster. Bring them inside before winter to prevent cracking.
- Wooden whiskey half-barrels look attractive and can stay out all winter.
- Tin cans have a funky esthetic—old olive-oil tins look great planted with herbs.
- I've seen and, in some cases, used wheelbarrows, hiking boots, small rowboats, watering troughs and old metal milking jugs as containers for plants. You are only limited by your joie de vivre.

Vines

Situate vines, peas, beans and kiwi fruit on the north side of the garden so they don't shade other plants. Plant vines beside existing fences or make temporary supports, using netting, chicken wire or string strung between sticks you have hammered into the ground. Or pound three sticks into the earth and tie them together into a tepee shape. Plant pole beans or peas or indeterminate tomatoes around them. As the tomatoes grow, fasten them to the stick supports (see A Good Stake, page 39).

Peas are planted on the east side of the bed so that the carrots, arugula and mâche can maximize the sunlight. Deep-rooted carrots bring up minerals, peas fix nitrogen and when the borage blooms it attracts pollinating insects.

Plants that Quickly Go to Seed

Spinach, some lettuce, arugula and radishes grow flowers and make seeds in record time. Slow their tendency to bolt by growing them in the shade of taller plants.

Fast-Growing Crops

Re-sow fast-growing crops, like radishes, arugula, cilantro and cress, as soon as the first crop has sprouted. Choose spots next to taller plants, vines and potatoes. Once the taller plants have leafed out and matured, the fast-growers will be finished and out of the way.

Cut-and-Come-Again Leafy Greens

Cut-and-come-again crops, such as lettuce, kale, spinach, sorrel and arugula, can be harvested again and again. Plant them in a row or a block and do not thin. As they start growing, use a pair of scissors to shear off the tops for a tasty salad. You can keep repeating this until the frost irrevocably kills them. Shearing down quick-to-bolt crops like arugula, spinach and some lettuces helps to keep them from going to seed, and prolongs the life of the plants.

Early-Spring Perennials

Plant sorrel, lovage and chives in a warm spot on the south side of a wall or building to get a jump on your early-spring harvest. By July, these crops have hopelessly gone to seed unless you are vigilant about cutting them back. When they start growing flowers, cut off the flower heads or the entire stalk to prolong the harvest. Situate more of these plants in a cooler spot, in the open garden or next to taller plants where they will get some shade, and you should be able to continue their harvest all summer and into the fall.

Tall Edibles

Grow the tallest plants, like sunflowers, beans and lovage, on the north side of the garden so that they don't shade the rest of the plants. Most plants grow better in full sun.

Underplanting—Unlike Underwear, You Want to See It

Underplant everything, even plants grown in pots. And plant your crops close enough together so that when fully grown there is no bare soil visible—this will conserve soil moisture and discourage weeds. Surround taller plants with ground-hugging choices like lettuce and arugula, quick-growing crops like radish and cress, or cut-and-come-again greens (see above).

Underplanting acts as living mulch, keeping the soil moist and covering bare soil, stopping undesirable weeds from moving in. Underplanting is a way to diversify the plant neighbourhood, keeping pests on their toes as they try to figure out where the food they want to eat is planted.

Unlike the expensive bark mulch (dead mulch) you buy from the garden centre, living mulch is relatively cheap because you can grow it from seed, and you can eat it too. Living mulch contributes to the overall health of the soil by encouraging soil organisms, conserving water and adding nutrients to the soil when it rots. In my gardens, underplanting is customary.

Maximize Your Space

Sign up for a community plot to extend your growing space, or celebrate because you have a backyard and front yard to grow food.

Layer it On

Make use of plant layers in your garden, patio or balcony to increase your space to grow more food. Group plants that grow in a similar way into tiers. For example, a top layer consists of trees like apple, cherry and plum and tall shrubs like saskatoon berry. Smaller shrubs, such as blueberries, currants, Jerusalem artichoke, rhubarb and horseradish, form a second layer. A third layer includes mid-sized annual flowers, herbs and vegetables like calendula, greens, brassicas, oregano, dill and loads of others. Ground covers like chickweed, dandelion, thyme, mint and clover form a fourth layer, and climbers like beans, peas and kiwi make a fifth.

Stack 'em Up

Stacking your plants helps you take advantage of plant layers. For example, when planting trees, first take into account their eventual spread and height. Add shrubs and perennials, vegetables and herbs beneath them and around them to take advantage

Garlic is up and growing the minute the snow melts. Short-season radishes will be done with by the time the beans grow up to take over the space.

of the light afforded by immature growth. Vines can be supported by shrubs or trees or even tall perennials. Annuals, vegetables, herbs and flowers need the most sun and are grown in the light-filled spaces between permanent plants, while ground covers round out the mix, covering up bare soil.

In my garden, I grow annual food and herb crops in raised beds, pots and bright spaces between herbaceous perennials, shrubs and trees.

Make the Most of Multiple Plant Features

When choosing plants for your garden, think about their multiple uses. Rhubarb, for example, provides food for humans, its leaves make great mulch that can be composted into life-giving humus, its tall stature provides shade to crops that like it cool, and the flowers do a fabulous job of attracting insects. Listing a plant's attributes helps you to decide how to best incorporate it into your garden.

Sustainable Garden Design

Sustainable gardens are designed around plant functions and how they interact with other plants and the environment. Look to nature for inspiration. Your garden is a dynamic community that is always changing. As the tree canopy fills out and the garden matures, some plants will be shaded out, while others will adapt to the new lower light conditions.

After a few years of nutrient accumulation from nitrogen fixers, deep-rooted plants and mulch makers, the soil will have built up enough to ensure plants get all the nutrition they need just from their annual cycles of leaf drop and renewal. The plants complement each other, keeping the soil moist and reducing evaporation, so there is little need for you to water. Shrubs and trees provide homes for wildlife and food for all of us.

In your garden, you can achieve this ideal by growing mostly perennial food plants. Of course, you still want to grow lettuce, tomatoes and beans, so provide growing space for your annual plants in raised beds, containers, pots, greenhouses in open areas, your deck, the south side of a building and between trees and shrubs.

CHAPTER 3

Choose the Right Crops

NORTHERN SUMMERS ARE SHORT AND FLEETING, AND— EXCEPT FOR A SINGLE WEEK IN JULY—EVEN SHORTER ON HEAT

I was surprised to discover the first time I looked through a seed catalogue that carrots are not simply carrots, that there are many types. Plant varieties specialize and adapt themselves to distinct ecological niches. There are short, fat carrots to grow in clay soils and longer, skinnier carrots for lighter soils.

Many plant species offer hundreds of varieties. These modifications have evolved so that plants can successfully grow in varying areas of the world, where soil, climate and the number of frost-free days differ. The most exciting distinction for northern gardeners is that some varieties require less time to mature. Choosing edibles that ripen quickly allows the short-season gardener a much better chance of harvesting a crop.

Some Plants Need a Little Help

This doesn't mean you can't grow heat-loving crops too, such as peppers or tomatoes, which need longer to mature. Plants that take more than 65 days to ripen or those that require lots of heat just need extra help from you. Increase and trap heat around them by:

- Starting crops indoors, under lights, to get a jump on the season.
- Sowing seeds of warm-weather crops, which need warmer soil to germinate, indoors or in the greenhouse where the soil is toastier, transplanting them outside after they germinate.
- Growing warm-weather crops all season in greenhouses or cold frames, or under row covers or another protection against frosty nights.
- Identifying and making use of warm microclimates. Even during times of the year when there is no frost, temperatures in the north are chillier. Plants grow slower in cooler weather and take longer to germinate. So take advantage of any protected spots your landscape offers.

Get Educated

Whenever I take up a new interest, I become completely obsessed by it, reading everything I can get my hands on. Sometimes I take lessons or join a club to meet and talk with others about my new consuming passion.

Books

The library near me in Dawson Creek was small, with the gardening-book collection occupying only a couple of shelves. I took out every one of those books several times, reading every word, soaking up the knowledge and experience imparted by generations of northern and Canadian gardeners. Eventually, I began to understand the meaning of "winterkill," "hardy bulb" and "frost tender."

Catalogues

Browse seed catalogues—many seed companies send them out for free—or, better yet, skip the paper waste and look at their selection online. See Resources for Northern Gardeners on my website, *northerngardenersalmanac.com*, for seed-company recommendations and links.

Garden Clubs

Join your local horticultural society or garden club. You'll meet knowledgeable, interesting people, and will also be privy to garden tours, informative lectures, meetings and plant sales…and you may even get free plants.

Internet

The web is a huge repository of gardening information, with access to plant, seed and bulb catalogues, gardening magazines, gardening podcasts, gardening discussions and gardening blogs. You can connect with people who live in the same city or on another continent—and just seeing what other people are growing, even if it's in a different climate, is eye-opening and fun.

Perennials, Biennials, Annuals…What's the Difference?

Knowing what types of plants you have helps you determine where to plant them, what the optimum harvest times are and when to expect flowers and seed. In northern gardens, some plants take a long time to grow flowers. Last year, my sage flowered for the first time—I was flabbergasted because, despite its being obvious, I had forgotten that the plant has flowers and sets seed. Basil is another plant, due to the short growing season, I have never seen flower.

Perennials

Perennials live longer than two years, take more time than annuals to reach maturity and generally don't produce a decent harvest for three to even five years in a short-season climate. A one-time investment, perennials provide food without requiring the tedious work of seeding plants every year. They can be herbaceous (meaning stems and leaves die back to the ground annually) or woody evergreen or deciduous plants.

Biennials

Biennials die after two years—spending their first year growing leaves and roots, the second producing flowers and seed.

Annuals

Annuals live for one growing season, flowering and setting seed within the same year.

Tender Perennials

In the harsh conditions of a cold-climate garden, many tender perennials—plants that would live ongoingly in a milder environment but are too delicate to survive the rigours of the northern winter—are treated as annuals.

Biennial parsley grows leaves the first year; in the second year it flowers, sets seed and then dies.

Many cold-climate gardeners throw tender perennials away at the end of the season, starting over with fresh stock the following spring. If you have space and patience, though, you can keep some of these plants alive on a windowsill or dormant in a cool basement during winter.

Rosemary is a great example of a tender perennial that adapts readily to the environment inside your house. Many other herbs, vegetables and flowers also fall into this category but not all of them are suitable candidates for bringing indoors. Review Edibles for Short-Season Gardening (beginning on page 88) for specifics on what tender perennials can benefit from an indoor hiatus during the cold season.

Hardy Annuals

Hardy annuals reseed themselves year after year—once you plant them in your garden, you will always have them. In northern gardens, edible hardy annuals include borage, calendulas and violets or pansies.

Consider Hybrid versus Open-Pollinated Seed

Flashy hybrids are the latest in technological engineering, while open-pollinated or heritage seeds use their own genes to adapt to the changing environment—without the need for help from scientists.

Plant borage once and it will self-seed so vigorously you will never need to plant it again. All parts of a borage plant are edible—and its flowers attract pollinating insects like bees.

Hybrid Seed

Hybrid seed is selectively cross-pollinated by hand, in a lab, to achieve certain characteristics like bigger fruit. These cross-pollinated plants are inbred to produce a stable, standardized plant. The plants are crossbred to produce seeds known as F1 hybrids. Plants grown from F1 hybrid seeds exhibit what is known as hybrid vigour—they have a higher yield than their inbred parents. Plants from F1 hybrids are homogeneous: they all look the same.

Many flowers are designed by nature to aid pollination by specific insects. Hybridizers altering plants, usually to increase yield, can change the plant so radically that it becomes difficult for insects to pollinate it.

Seed collected from F1 hybrid plants produces F2 hybrid plants. F2 hybrid plants are heterogeneous—they will not have the same vigour or appearance as their F1 hybrid parents.

If you choose F1 hybrid seed, you will have to keep buying it to get the equivalent plant. I've never collected and planted seed from F1 hybrid plants. Given the unpredictable nature of F2 hybrid plants grown from seed collected from F1 hybrid plants, I'm unsure that it is worthwhile.

Open-Pollinated, Heirloom or Heritage Seed

"Open pollinated," "heirloom" or "heritage" refers to seed developed before the advent of modern agriculture. These seeds have been collected by gardeners or farmers from plants grown in their gardens or on their farms. Over time, the plants have responded to their environment, producing seed and plants specifically adapted to their local conditions. You can enjoy this same advantage by collecting seed from open-pollinated plants in your own garden.

I like the idea of growing plants from open-pollinated seed. It's appealing to me that over time the seed I collect will have evolved to suit the conditions in my garden. Read more under Collect Seed (page 79).

I source any other seed I need from smaller businesses, which I like to support. As a bonus, these small places often sell seed of little-known but valuable plant varieties that big companies can't be bothered with.

Decide What to Plant

Natural or homemade microclimates in your garden dictate what you can grow.

Cool-Weather Crops

Started outside after the snow melts and soil is workable, cool-weather crops are what you will primarily grow in your garden.

Root crops can be left in the garden over winter and harvested again the following spring. Their biennial or perennial nature means that despite freezing they still come through winter unscathed and edible. Leave some biennial carrots and beets in the ground, letting them flower and go to seed. Collect the seeds to sow next year. Dig up potatoes in spring, transplanting them to a fresh place in the garden for another harvest. And, yes, you can eat these overwintered root crops for dinner too.

Greens like kale, mustard greens, beet greens, cabbage and Brussels sprouts taste even better after they have been touched by frost. By November, or earlier in zone 2, the ground is frozen and you will be digging your vegetables, if you're lucky, out of the snow. Eventually, the snow packs down like the base of a ski hill and then even a pickaxe won't help you get to your vegetables until spring arrives.

Perennial vegetables like asparagus, rhubarb, sorrel and other herbs are hardy and reliable. They come back every spring, providing a dependable source of food.

Onions, beets and Swiss chard love cool weather.

Short-Season Crops

Vegetables that require only 30 days or less to mature—cress, radish, arugula and many more varieties of greens—are called short-season crops. In addition, greens that take longer to mature—like spinach, lettuce, kale and collards—can still be considered short season because they can be harvested as baby greens before maturity. They can be snipped again and again (in my garden, I cut them repeatedly until they're finished off by frost), providing an ongoing supply of fresh, succulent leaves for the kitchen without the need to replant.

Warm-Weather Crops

Warm-weather crops need to be fussed over and encouraged to grow in order to produce. Plant them outside when the soil warms up in mid-June. If you wish to harvest heat-loving crops that take longer than 65 days to mature, you will need a greenhouse, cold frame or row cover to protect them from being killed by frost before harvest time (see Crop Covers, page 39).

Some summers, when—week after week—grey skies, unrelenting rain and lack of warmth or sunlight slow the growth of warm-weather crops to a glacial pace, harvesting ripe zucchini or a red tomato seems an impossible goal. Many people, fed up with unpredictable weather, grow all their warm-weather crops inside a greenhouse (see Greenhouse, page 40).

Tomatoes, cucumbers, peppers, summer squash, beans, annual herbs and flowers are some of the crops that need warm soil to grow.

While beans are a warm-weather crop; fennel (right) is fine in the cold.

Start Planting Your Edible Garden

There are many ways to fill up your garden—and some need not cost much…or anything at all.

Get Divisions

Ask friends, even strangers, for divisions of their plants. (See Make More Plants, page 78). Once, on a walk through my new neighbourhood, I stopped to talk to a gardener, expressing admiration for her garden and choice of plants. In no time, she had invited me into her yard, given me a shovel and instructed me to help myself to whatever I fancied and to take lots of it. I lugged three bagfuls of plants home.

Once established, perennials like rhubarb, oregano and sorrel, keep growing and growing and growing—gardeners are forced to cut them back or divide them up and toss the extras onto the compost pile if they can't pass them on.

Sow Seeds

I grow all my plants from seed—starting plants from seed is inexpensive and simple. You have access to greater numbers and varieties of plants if you choose to grow from seed. With so many available cultivars of each species, developed for specific garden niches, it is easy to pick the right one to suit your garden's growing conditions.

Buy Seedlings (or Not)

Seedlings are only available in nurseries for the most popular vegetables and flowers, and usually only a couple of varieties of each vegetable is offered. Buying enough seedlings to fill your garden is expensive. If you want just one of something, though, or are not up to the work that growing perennials entails, then go ahead and buy a seedling or a few.

Add Edible Flowers and Herbs

Some herbs are grown for their flowers, or, conversely, flowers are grown for their herb-like qualities. Edible flowers like borage and nasturtium can be used as a garnish in salads, summer drinks, dips, sandwiches and desserts. Use lots to pretty up a plate of food.

Herbs provide inimitable flavour and I cannot imagine a garden without them: Basil, the typical accompaniment to tomatoes, brings the taste of Italy to the north. Mint, a plant that practically grows itself, complements everything from roast lamb to sweets, tea and curries. Grow marjoram and oregano for Italian and Greek dishes, sage for poultry, and horseradish for roast beef. Bulb fennel, sorrel, lovage, onions, garlic, parsley and cress are grown and eaten as vegetables in my home.

Most herbs are perennial and easy to grow in northern gardens. After the initial output for seeds or seedling starts, you have little to do but harvest the results. Why pay good money for bunches of wilted parsley and cilantro or, even worse, those over-priced factory sweepings that are passed off as dried herbs in supermarkets? Many garden herbs—such as basil and parsley—retain most of their flavour and freshness when frozen and can be available for your use in the kitchen all winter.

Incorporating herbs and flowers into your cooking enables you to produce meals that rival those served in expensive restaurants—without the overpriced bill.

Harvest Edible Wild Food

As you garden, chances are you'll also find native edibles growing alongside your crops, somewhere in your yard or in the spaces that surround it. I'm grateful for this free food and harvest it along with the vegetables and fruits I grow.

Native Berries

My second childhood home in Canada was on BC's Sunshine Coast. My mother went mad for blackberries there. Every August, we braved the thorns to gather bucket-loads to be made into jam and pies. Our blackberry-stained fingers and faces gave away the fact that more than half our pickings were conveyed to our mouths rather than the buckets.

Alas, blackberries don't grow up north. Instead, we have saskatoons and, if we are lucky, blueberries growing in our hedgerows. The bonus is that neither has thorns, but they too stain my fingers blue-black.

Other wild northern shrubs with edible berries include raspberry, thimbleberry, cranberry, gooseberry and currant. MacKinnon, Pojar and Coupé's *Plants of Northern British Columbia* is a great resource on native edibles.

Apart from feeding humans, allowing wild berries into your garden provides extra food for birds—and they may even leave your domesticated berries alone. As a bonus, all that pecking birds do in the garden turns over and aerates the top layer of soil; also, their droppings fertilize it. Birds help disperse seeds, spreading plants around the garden and bringing in new ones.

Dandelions and Other Delicious Weeds

Dandelions (*Taraxacum officinale*) are one of the first flowers in northern gardens. They are an important early source of nectar for domestic and wild bees. Every spring, bees wake up looking for a good meal—allowing dandelions into your garden encourages bees to hang around and pollinate your other plants.

Every May–June, when the earth comes alive and plants are frantically growing, I look for baby dandelion leaves in my garden to pick for my first spring salads. Young leaves are the tenderest, and a simple vinaigrette with a dash of mustard and salt and pepper is all that's required to enhance their flavour.

Unlike other spreadacious weeds, dandelions are not on the invasive list. While they do spread rapidly by seed, grazing sheep and cows love to eat the entire plant and tend to keep it generally under control. The long taproot brings up nutrients from deep below, making the whole plant very nutritious for both animals and humans. Dandelions are an excellent addition to your compost. Get them before they go to seed, or pull off the seed heads to send to the landfill compost.

Other edible weeds to encourage include lamb's quarters (*Chenopodium album*), pineappleweed (*Matricaria discoidea*), chickweed (*Stellaria media*) and plantain (*Plantago major*)—in addition to providing human food, the flowers and scents of these plants attract beneficial insects. Plus, they cover the ground like a shallow-rooted living mulch, protecting the soil from erosion, keeping it moist and maintaining a good home for essential soil organisms.

Choices, Choices, Choices

Starting small with a few key plants gives you confidence to try more with each new season. Daunting endeavours like growing plants from seed will become almost effortless. The more you discover about plants, the more you want to know and the more you want to grow. My plant collection is an ever-expanding compendium of species from many genera. The plant world is huge, its diversity enormous, and you can't help but be intrigued.

CHAPTER 4

How to Plant

RIGHT PLANT, RIGHT PLACE: DECIDING WHAT TO PLANT WHERE...AND WHEN

I dislike planning, and prefer to think that spontaneity allows for a fuller and more enriching life—but it's not always so in the garden.

I recommend that you make a rough sketch of your vegetable garden every year, writing down what you plant in each area. Pay attention to height, spread and whether the plant is permanent or seasonal; and, most importantly, take note of what family the plant belongs to, as this is integral to annual crop rotation. I spend a few minutes with pencil and paper scribbling up my plan every spring before I plant, and archive all my garden maps so that I can refer back to them in years to come.

Crop Rotation Won't Make You Dizzy

Crop rotation is the most important way to reduce disease and insect infestations in your garden. Plants in the same family are susceptible to the same problems and pests. Typically, diseases and insects take more than a year to develop. Rotating the plants means that the host plants—where specific bugs develop—are not present in the soil the following year; without their host plants, the insects and disease-causing microbes die. Crop rotation is simple if you follow these steps:

1. List what plants you want to grow, grouping them into their plant families.
2. Sketch a rough map of your garden, dividing it into sections.
3. Plant each section with a specific family.
4. The following year, refer back to this map, drawing up a new one that rotates each plant family into a different spot. Plants are typically rotated on a three-year schedule. Here's an example: In Bed A, plant Fabaceae or Leguminosae (legumes) the first year, Solanaceae (potatoes) the second year and Brassicaceae (brassicas) the third year. In the fourth year, you can plant legumes again.
5. Make a new map/plan every year, keeping it so that you can refer back to it.

Every plant listed in Edibles for Short-Season Gardening (beginning on page 88) is categorized under its family name to help you plan your crop rotation.

How Perennials and Biennials Fit into the Rotation Plan

Now you know to rotate annual plants on a three-year plan, allowing two years before planting the same annual crop back into the same bed. But what about perennials and biennials?

Because perennials are permanent plantings, I choose different companion plants every year to put near them, treating this space as another bed in which to rotate annual crops. So while the perennial plants stay where they live, the annuals planted around them change in a three-year rotation.

Biennials last for two years, and it's no problem for them to remain in the same spot for this period. But be sure to plant new crops in that area for each of the subsequent two years, to keep with the crop-rotation strategy.

What to Do about the Greenhouse

I plant tomatoes, basil and peppers in my greenhouse every year, so instead of practising crop rotation there I reduce the possibility of disease and pests by replacing the soil periodically, trading soil in the greenhouse with soil from the garden. I find the best time to do this is in the fall, once the garden has died back and I'm less busy.

When to Start Growing

Different crops start growing at different times, depending on where they are situated in the garden and their own idiosyncratic cycles.

Spring to My Favourite Time of Year

You know spring has finally arrived when the snow starts melting in earnest, dripping off the roof, turning to slush in the driveway and eventually running in rivers down south-facing slopes. At last the ground is visible around the receding snowpack; soon enough frost will have melted out of the ground to turn the soil into mud.

Spring is coming but winter still plunges the mercury below zero every night. In town, on the south side of the street, the buds on the mayday trees are almost bursting; at lunchtime, the sunshine feels hot. Gradually, the snow is gone but it's only the middle of April—everywhere is still coloured by bare chocolate-brown branches of deciduous trees, beige grass and the remains of plants the colour of coffee, caramel and sienna. We northerners call the weeks of anticipation before the world starts turning green "the brown season."

Green is the Colour

After seven long months of a brown-and-white landscape, my colour-starved eyes and antagonized soul eagerly revel in the sight of revived green grass and new leaves.

Once dormancy is broken, plants grow fast. Plants that take weeks or even months to appear in southern gardens grow, flower and produce seed in mere days. In zone 2,

Some very welcome new growth.

the growing season may last as little as 12 weeks. The seasons get squished together, as spring, summer and fall plants all rush to complete their growing cycle.

Gardening Zone 2

While the summer season may be short, each summer day is longer than that farther south. This extended daylight is a saviour for the far-northern gardener—the longer days mean more sunlight and more growing time for plants, which respond at break-neck speeds. You can practically see the plants growing in their headlong rush to produce flowers and seed before being killed by frost.

Gardening Zone 3

In zone 3, summer may be marginally longer, but its days are shorter than those far-ther north. There is less sunlight, which means less time for plants to grow each day. Plants do not have the exceptional fast growth they have in zone 2. This is the most significant difference I've noticed between my zone-2 garden in the BC Peace and my zone-3 garden in Prince George.

Countryside versus Cityside

Another visible difference is a result of the Urban Heat Island effect. The concentra-tion of concrete buildings, sidewalks and roads in the city make it hotter than the sur-rounding countryside. The temperature difference may be enough to increase your zone rating…and to induce you to try plants rated for this warmer zone.

Gardeners in the city of Prince George plant crops earlier than I do—and their plants mature quicker than mine. Some gardeners even grow winter squash and corn, plants I don't bother with because the heat in my country garden is insufficient.

Plant Cool Crops and Warm Crops

In northern gardens, take advantage of natural cool and hot times:
- Plant cool-weather crops and perennials as early as possible—as soon as the ground is dry enough to be worked.
- Plant warm-weather crops a week or two after the last frost date, sometime in mid-June, to take advantage of warmer soil and mild nights. Planting warm-weather crops in cold soil increases the possibility that they will rot.

These guidelines are just that, though, because in zone 2 what the calendar says doesn't really count. Case in point: one July 1 long weekend, we had all our living-room furniture out on the lawn, with our houseplants lined up alongside the house, while we refinished the wooden floor inside. It took us the entire weekend to sand and apply several coats of stain to the floor before we could take everything back inside. One night, the mercury dipped below zero, with the frost killing the tops of most of the garden plants and burning some of the houseplants. Amazingly, although in ret-rospect hardly surprising since none of their roots were killed, all the plants grew new leaves—both the houseplants and those in the garden.

To get a jump on spring, start seeds indoors before the ground thaws outdoors.

Start Seeds Indoors Under Lights

Cheat nature by getting a jump on the season—start your plants indoors.

What to Start Indoors

Some plants you want to grow in your garden may not flower or produce fruit before frost unless you start them from seed and continue growing them indoors for a few weeks before transplanting outside. Perennials and annuals that require more than 65 days to mature need to be started indoors. (For specific plant information, see Edibles for Short-Season Gardening, beginning on page 88.)

Most of the seeds you germinate indoors will be transplanted outside as soon as they start developing their true leaves, usually within a couple of weeks. The first leaves that sprout from a seed are generic and called the cotyledon or seed leaves. Subsequent leaves are true leaves and differ according to the characteristics of the specific plant. Eventually, you will be able to recognize plants by their true leaves.

What You Need to Make a Grow Station

Growing seedlings indoors mimics outdoor growing conditions. Here's what you need:

- Fluorescent light box
- Fluorescent tubes (two per light box)
- Timer
- Extension cord
- Table
- Pulleys
- String
- Shallow containers—punch holes in the bottom for drainage
- Under trays
- Plant mister
- Watering can
- Seed-starting or regular potting mix—I've used both and not noticed a perceptible difference
- Seeds

Assembling the Grow Station

- Wire fluorescent light boxes to extension cords by twisting the same-coloured wires together. If you are having trouble, ask the staff at the hardware store to help you.
- Suspend the light box from the ceiling, using a pulley that allows you to raise it above your plants as they grow.
- Plug the extension cord into a timer so it can turn the light box on and off.
- Place a table beneath the light for the seedlings.

Maintaining the Grow Station

- Set the timer to keep the lights on for 12–16 hours a day. Like you, plants need a rest at night to grow properly.
- As soon as your annual seeds have sprouted, put them beneath the lights. Annuals need heat to germinate (see Starting Annuals from Seed Indoors, page 64). Perennials and biennials don't need extra heat to germinate, so place them beneath the lights as soon as you've sown them.
- Lower the light box so it is directly above the seedlings—get it as close as you can to the leaves.
- As the plants grow, raise the light box in increments, always remembering to keep it close to the leaves. Keeping the lights as near as possible to the leaves stops the plants from becoming leggy, helping them grow like they would in outside conditions.
- Change your lights every season. Fluorescent light tubes diminish in intensity over time. Get the best possible light by starting each year with new bulbs.

> **Lights for Growing Seedlings**
>
> *Any cheap fluorescent lights are all you need for healthy seedlings. They emit light from the blue-green area of the spectrum, ideal for growing leaves and stems. Expensive grow lights emit light from the red area of the spectrum that plants use to grow flowers—you don't need these lights, as your seedlings will be outside when they are ready to grow flowers.*

Sowing Seeds Indoors

- Fill containers with soil mix, tamping it down.
- Water them, letting any excess drain through.
- Read the back of the seed packet—many seeds only need to be pressed down onto the top of the soil; others may have to be covered.
- If you are covering the seeds, use as little soil as possible—no more than twice the diameter of the seed. Be careful not to plant seeds too deep, as they may not sprout.
- Mist seeds gently until wet.
- Monitor daily for dryness, letting the seeds dry out completely before re-watering them. Water too much and you will drown them or possibly grow a fungus called damping off, which will kill your seedlings (see Damping Off on page 76 for more on this).
- As the seedlings grow, pinch out the terminal leaves to encourage side branching and pinch the terminal buds of the side branches. All this pinching encourages your plants to grow lush, sturdy and healthy.

Label seeds you plant in pots to grow indoors. Many times I've skipped this step only to agonize later over what the seedlings are.

When to Start Indoors

Deciding when to germinate seeds is a balancing game—start them too early and you waste time and energy transplanting them to bigger pots before the garden is ready to receive them; start them too late and they won't mature in time for a good harvest.

Starting Perennials from Seed Indoors

Perennials and biennials are prime candidates for starting early indoors. They grow slower than annuals and don't need heat to germinate. Place your containers of sown seed directly beneath the grow lights. In zones 2 and 3, start your perennials in late March. I have successfully grown lovage, oregano, marjoram, rosemary, thyme, asparagus, sorrel and a variety of perennial flowers from seed.

Some Seeds Need Help to Germinate

All seeds need water to germinate and sometimes we need to get past their "coat" to make this happen. The coat is a layer of protection around the seed, keeping it from germinating until conditions are favourable. The seed coat needs to split open, allowing water to be absorbed by the seed so it can germinate. Seed coats of some species are so hard they need to be scratched, a process called scarification, before they will crack open to allow water to penetrate the seed.

Seeds of other species need to be stratified, which means they have to undergo a cold period of an hour to several months (depending on the seed) before the coat splits open.

The plants you are likely to be growing probably do not need to be scarified or stratified, but read the back of the seed packet to make sure.

Starting Annuals from Seed Indoors

I start onion seeds, tomatoes and peppers in late March. Squash, cucumbers, parsley and nasturtiums are started early May; I transplant these outside after they sprout.

Annuals may need additional warmth to germinate: increase the heat by sprouting them on a sunny south-facing windowsill, on top of a heat register or, like I do, next to a wood stove. After they have germinated, I transfer them to the growing station to increase their light and grow them on.

Why It's Better to Sow Most Seeds Directly Outside

With quick-maturing varieties of seeds widely available, it is not necessary to start most plants indoors. Despite our efforts to provide grow lights and pinch out terminal buds, plants grown from seeds directly planted in the garden are healthier. They don't suffer from transplant shock and instead can get used to the climate and soil from the

SOW SIMPLE COLD FRAME

A minimalist cold frame can be constructed with a single sheet of exterior-grade plywood if you measure and cut carefully. You'll finish with a back, front, two ends and a shelf. Measuring five feet wide, this portable frame can shelter a sizeable crop of cold-season veggies from winter's winds.

Tools:

Wood clamps
Circular saw or handsaw
Drill
Carpenter's square
Screwdriver

Materials:

Carpenter's glue
White latex paint and paint brush

Hardware:

About fifty #6 × ¾-in. round-head galvanized screws
About one hundred and fifty #8 × 1½-in. flat-head galvanized screws
Four 4-in. galvanized door hinges, with screws
Two sheets ¼-in. Plexiglas acrylic glazing, 37⅝ inch × 30⅜ inch
Eight 3-in. corner braces
Two 3-in. bolts and nuts (optional)

Lumber:

One sheet 4 × 8-ft. exterior grade ¼-in. plywood
Eight feet 1 × 2-inch lumber
2 × 2-inch lumber (see cutting instructions)

Cut the following rough lengths from 2 × 2-inch lumber to use as inside frames:

Front frames

Cut one 60 in. bottom
Cut one 60 in., bevel to fit against top edge
Cut two 8 in. sides

Back frames

Cut one 60 in. bottom
Cut one 60 in., bevel to fit top
Cut two 20 in. sides

Side frames

Cut two 32 in. bottoms
Cut two 34 in. tops

Lid frames

Cut four 34¾ in.
Cut four 30⅜ in.

Handles (optional)

Cut two 6 in.

....

Shelf (optional)

Cut four 8-in. 2 × 2-in. scraps to use as shelf ledge

Lid props (optional)

Cut two 1 × 2 in. × 4 ft.

For Base:

Paving stones or bricks (30 linear ft.)

1. Cut the plywood using the dimensions provided. Note that three scrap pieces will also be produced.

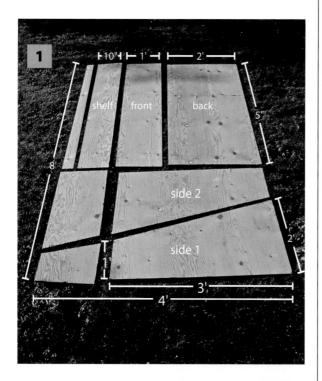

2. For extra strength use exterior carpenter's glue prior to screwing into place. Begin with the back piece and attach the corresponding frame pieces to frame the interior edges of the back panel. Drill and screw in place using flat-head screws (pre-drill holes to avoid splitting lumber). Repeat the same procedure on the front piece using the corresponding frame pieces. Attach the frame pieces to the top and bottom interior edges of each side panel, leaving room at each end to allow it to fit against the front and back interior framing. Attach handles (optional). Attach each side first to the back panel (corner to corner) and then to front panel.

3. To make lids, attach corresponding lid frame pieces to form two equal rectangles ($37^5/_8 \times 30^3/_8$ inch). Reinforce inside corners with corner brackets. Attach Plexiglas by drilling and securing to top of lid frame with round-head screws. Fit lids to top of cold frame and attach two hinges to each lid and against the back outside edge.

4. Attach the shelf piece by notching the corners and securing it to a ledge created by screwing small pieces of 2×2-inch lumber to the inside back and sides. The shelf will create valuable space in your cold frame and it's handy for trays of seedlings.

5. If using, attach props to the front of your cold frame with a bolt and nut. Position a screw (top extended ¼ in.) on the outside bottom edge of the lid (centred) and drill holes in 2-inch increments along the rod.

6. As an option, paint the inside of your assembled cold frame white to reflect the sunlight onto plants.

7. The finished cold frame will be portable and should be set on blocks of concrete or bricks to protect the bottom from rot. Choose a south or south-east location for your cold frame with good drainage and adequate shelter. A wall or hedge that provides protection from winter winds in the north is ideal. Raise the top during the heat of the day and close it up again early enough in the afternoon to keep the heat in overnight. To protect your crops further during colder weather, insulate at night by covering your cold frame with burlap sacks or old blankets.

Below: A finished cold frame

ROW COVERS MADE EASY

This simple row cover uses flexible PVC pipe as bracing.

Materials:

Six 5 ft. lengths 1-inch PVC pipe
Twelve 1 ft. lengths rebar
One roll medium-weight polyethylene to cover
 (about 15 × 6 ft.)
Clamps, staples or heavy-duty tape

1. Push one pair of rebar pieces 6 inches into the ground 2 feet across the row. Press opposite ends of a length of the PVC pipe firmly in place over the top of the rebar, forming an arc. Repeat with each length of PVC pipe, spacing the arcs 18 inches apart.

2. Unroll the poly film and extend it lengthwise over the arcs along the entire length of your row. If it is not wide enough to cover the entire arc, overlap two lengths of poly film to form a complete cover.

3. Secure the plastic to the pipe with clamps, staples or heavy-duty tape. Place rocks along the outside lower edges of the plastic to prevent it from flapping and tearing. Be sure to leave enough plastic at either end to close the row cover at night or during cold weather. Raise the sides during the heat of the day and close it up again early enough in the afternoon to keep the heat in overnight.

Row covers should be easy to remove in order to water plants and prevent overheating on hot days.

Cold frame and row cover photographs and instructions from Sow Simple: 100+ Green and Easy Projects to Make Your Garden Awesome *by Christina Symons and John Gillespie (Harbour Publishing, 2012)*

𝒞oroplast 𝓡ow 𝒞overs

Another easy row cover can be fashioned from a cut sheet of Coroplast, a flexible product that lets light through. Bend it into a semi-circle shape and secure with 8-in. (20-cm) wooden posts or rebar, or score it lightly with a knife and fold to create a free-standing cover. Don't forget to cut pieces to cover the ends, too.

RECYCLED CLOCHES

Traditional French glass cloches (right), meant to be placed over a single seedling to keep it warm in early spring, are beautiful in the garden. But most northern gardeners will only need cloches for a week or two, before the plant outgrows the space, so it's more practical to repurpose as many cloches as needed from the recycling bin:

1. Slice the bottom or top off a large plastic pop bottle or milk jug.

2. Sink the cloche firmly into the soil so it doesn't blow away, or affix with a stick.

3. Remove the lid during the day to provide ventilation to the plant inside.

4. Remove when danger of frost has passed and seedling has outgrown the space.

AVERAGE LAST SPRING FREEZE AND FIRST FALL FREEZE

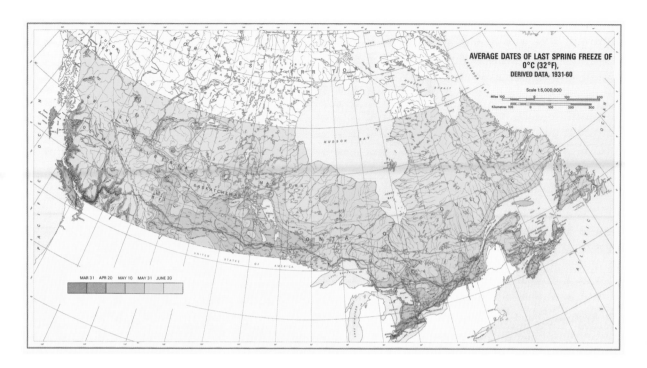

AVERAGE DATES OF LAST SPRING FREEZE OF
0°C (32°F),
DERIVED DATA, 1931-60

Scale 1:5,000,000

MAR 31   APR 20   MAY 10   MAY 31   JUNE 20

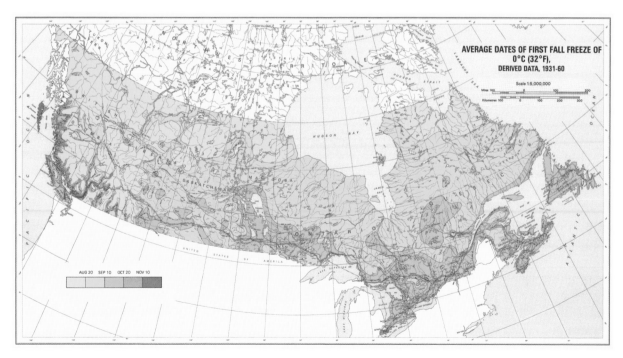

AVERAGE DATES OF FIRST FALL FREEZE OF
0°C (32°F),
DERIVED DATA, 1931-60

Scale 1:5,000,000

AUG 20   SEP 10   OCT 20   NOV 10

Agroclimatic Maps for Canada: Prepared by W.K. Sly, Cartography
by Soil Research Institute, Research Branch, Agriculture Canada.
Originally printed by the Surveys and Mapping Branch, Department
of Energy, Mines and Resources, Ottawa, 1977.

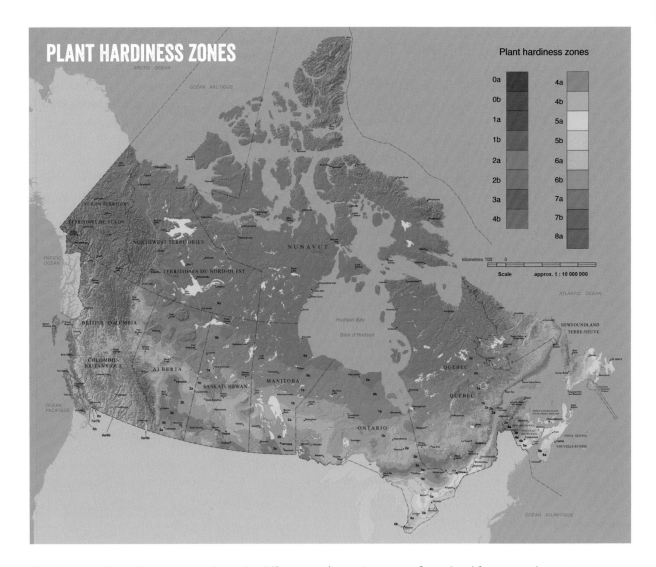

PLANT HARDINESS ZONES

Plant hardiness zones

0a	4a
0b	4b
1a	5a
1b	5b
2a	6a
2b	6b
3a	7a
4b	7b
	8a

kilometres 100   0
Scale   approx. 1 : 10 000 000

The Plant Hardiness Zones map outlines the different zones in Canada where various types of trees, shrubs and flowers will most likely survive. Natural Resources Canada's Canadian Forest Service scientists have used plant survival data and a wide range of climatic variables, including minimum winter temperatures, length of the frost-free period, summer rainfall, maximum temperatures, snow cover, January rainfall and maximum wind speed. They have also used modern climate mapping techniques and incorporated the effect of elevation.

The hardiness map is divided into nine major zones: the harshest is 0 and the mildest is 8. Relatively few plants are suited to zone 0. Subzones (e.g., 4a or 4b, 5a or 5b) are also noted in the map legend. These subzones are most familiar to Canadian gardeners.

Some significant local factors, such as micro-topography, amount of shelter and subtle local variations in snow cover, are too small to be captured on the map. Year-to-year variations in weather and gardening techniques can also have a significant impact on plant survival in any particular location.

For more details and a close-up view of your local plant hardiness zone, visit the atlas.agr.gc.ca/phz.

*The production of the new Plant Hardiness Zone Map was made possible through a collaborative effort by scientists at **Natural Resources Canada's Canadian Forest Service**, **Agriculture and Agri-Food Canada** and **Natural Resources Canada's National Atlas of Canada**.*

nanosecond they germinate. And directly sown plants often grow faster than their indoor-started counterparts.

Growing seedlings indoors is more work and mess for you. You have to be there every day, monitoring them for dryness and raising the lights. Plants sown inside need to be transplanted periodically, so their roots don't outgrow their containers. And they need to be acclimatized to the outside environment before they can be transplanted to the garden.

I grow as few seeds as possible indoors and like to get them outside quickly so I don't have to monitor them so intensely. Besides, with the fuss and bother, it's impractical to start all your plants indoors: Who has space to germinate hundreds of carrots?

For more information on the best way to start specific plants, see Edibles for Short-Season Gardening, beginning on page 88.

Planting Seeds Directly Outdoors

In zones 2 and 3, sow seeds of cool-weather crops as soon as the snow has melted and the ground is dry enough to work, usually sometime in May. Don't worry if it snows after you plant—think of snow as being an extra-cold watering.

Plant seeds for warm-weather crops in mid-June after the soil has warmed up. Germinating warm-weather crops outside is sometimes difficult. Even though the last frost date is long gone, night temperatures may still be less than 10C (50F). I've been known to dig up seeds, especially zucchini, to check out what they're doing down there, and sometimes even after a couple of weeks they still haven't sprouted. However, I've had great success direct-seeding other warm-weather crops such as beans outside. Nowadays, I germinate my zucchini and dill seeds in tiny pots indoors: they always sprout and I don't have to worry anymore about whether their non-germination is my fault or the seeds'. (Different seeds have different viability rates—read more about this in Edibles for Short-Season Gardening, beginning on page 88.)

Planting Outdoors Step by Step

1. *Trowel out slight depressions—about 1 cm (½ in) deep—in the soil. The depressions capture water, which soaks the seeds so they can absorb it, swell and sprout.*
2. *Lightly add water to the depressions, waiting for it to sink into the soil.*
3. *Read the back of the seed packet—very fine seeds only need to be pressed down onto the top of the soil, while others may have to be covered.*
4. *If you are covering the seeds, use as little soil as possible—no more than twice the diameter of the seed. Be careful not to plant seeds too deep, as they may not sprout*
5. *Lightly water the seeds, making sure they get wet.*
6. *Water them every day after the soil dries until they sprout.*
7. *After they sprout and start growing, thin them out, eating the thinnings.*

Know Your Frost Dates

Knowing your frost dates is useful because this helps you to decide when to plant your crops. Frost dates are an average point based on years of weather watching. As climate change may be affecting frost dates, use common sense when planting out young seedlings and seeds.

- In zone 2, the average last frost date is about the second week of June. The average first frost date is around the middle of August.
- In zone 3, the last frost date is usually the end of May. The first frost date is in the first half of September.

See the colour insert after page 64 for frost dates and zone maps.

Hardening Off: Get Your Seedlings Ready for the Big Bad World

In northern gardens, start acclimatizing seedlings to the outdoors in late May and early June. Transplant your seedlings into the garden after all danger of frost has passed. But before transplanting your coddled baby seedlings, you need to get them used to outdoor weather. Outdoors, the sunlight is many times brighter than the lights you use to grow your seedlings, the air is cooler and the winds cold and drying. The process of acclimatizing your seedlings is called "hardening off."

Allow at least a whole week to get your plants ready for the real world. Even though northern daytime temperatures in late May and early June can be relatively hot—up to 20C (68F)—nighttime temperatures are still apt to plunge below zero Celsius. Because of this, you need to bring your seedlings indoors or cover them every night—or risk losing them to a killing frost.

If you wait until after the last frost date to harden off your seedlings, you will be wasting valuable time the plants could be using to get acclimatized to the garden. If you don't bother to get your plants hardened off, they will most likely burn beneath the hot sun, dry out and/or get blown to bits by wind, and they may even die.

How to Harden Off Plants

1. *The first day, during midday, put your plants outside in a shady, sheltered spot. The east side of your house is ideal. Leave them out there for two hours maximum.*
2. *The next day, leave them outside in the same spot for four hours.*
3. *The third day and days after, gradually move them into the sunshine, leaving them out for longer and longer periods every day.*
4. *By the end of the week, they will be outside under full sunshine all day and loving it.*

Transplanted tomatoes and direct-seeded basil basking in the warmth of the greenhouse in June.

Transplanting Seedlings into a Greenhouse

I take my heat-loving seedlings (peppers and tomatoes) directly from my house to plant them in the greenhouse in late May through early June. They don't need to be hardened off because the greenhouse protects them from nasty weather, except severe freezing. I use jugs of water to provide additional warmth at night around each baby plant (see Heat Things Up in the Greenhouse, page 41). By this time of year, the weather is on a distinct warming trend, the days are longer, plants are growing fast and severe frost is unlikely.

CHAPTER 5

The Smart Way to Maintain Your Garden

YOU'VE PLANTED YOUR SEEDS…SO NOW WHAT? MOTHER NATURE WILL LEAD THE WAY

*T*he vegetables and fruit you plant in your garden, for the most part, are aliens, and require help from you to thrive. They need cushy soil, extra water and protection from frost, weeds and insects.

Get Equipped

When I started gardening, I had only an ancient hand-me-down spade and an equally decrepit wheelbarrow, both left behind by the previous owners of the house. At the time, I used my bare hands to dig holes for seedlings and my fingers to poke depressions in the soil for seeds. Since then, I've compiled a collection of basic tools to make gardening easier:

A hand trowel, spade and secateurs make gardening easier.

Wheelbarrow or Wheeled Cart: Use it to move garden litter to the compost pile and transport soil, heavy perennials and compost to your garden beds. I load mine up with garden tools, small plants, bulbs and a watering can. As I move around the garden, planting, watering, trimming, harvesting and removing weeds, my wheelbarrow fills up. When I'm done, I roll it over to the compost heap to drop off garden debris and finally to the kitchen door with any crops I've harvested.

Hand trowel: Very helpful for digging out depressions for seeds, making holes for bulbs and seedlings, and uprooting weeds.

Spade: Invaluable for planting big perennials, shrubs and trees. Or use it for turning compost and shovelling it out of the bin onto the garden, levelling soil and other large projects.

Gloves: You'll need gloves to keep your hands warm in early spring and late fall. I wear old winter gloves or mitts—they are thicker and warmer than gardening gloves. Gloves protect your hands from sharp thorns and slow down or prevent the formation of blisters and calluses, especially in spring before hands adapt to constant wheelbarrowing, spading and trowelling.

Watering Can: For irrigating seedlings, seeds, pots and spot-watering thirsty plants in the garden.

Hose: To irrigate the garden and compost heap.

Spray Attachment: A spray is gentler on your plants than a direct blast from the hose, and you can use it to direct the water around the plants' roots.

Leaf Rake: Rake up lawn cuttings or the leaves from your driveway and paths—then throw it all onto the compost heap.

Secateurs: You'll use these for deadheading flowers, cutting back excess plant growth, pruning woody perennials and harvesting crops.

Hacksaw: I appropriated this from my husband's tool collection when I needed something stronger than secateurs to cut back shrub branches and saw annoying aspen tree roots in half before attempting to pull them up.

Working with the Biggest Weeds

Aspen (a.k.a. poplar, Populus tremuloides*) is common in cooler areas of North America. The BC Peace is overrun with this giant weed that spreads by root sprouts. Each sprout is a clone of the original tree, and one plant can populate several acres of land. Clonal colonies of aspen are easily distinguished in autumn, when their leaves change colour at the same time. Aspens' shallow roots grow quickly, infiltrating the garden and sucking up nutrients and water. The roots sprout leaves that are easy to see. I dig around the sprout with my fingers, cut the root in half with a hacksaw (the roots are usually never more than a couple of inches below the surface of the soil) and effortlessly pull out as much as I can.*

Quench Plant Thirst

Water helps plants take up nutrients from the soil, facilitates photosynthesis and keeps essential soil organisms alive. Sustainable gardens are designed to be self-sufficient, so the watering the gardener needs to do is reduced or eliminated.

Throw Away the Sprinkler

Hand-water with a watering can, or a hose equipped with a spray attachment that can be shut off between plants as you drag it around the garden. Hand-watering your plants gives you the control to direct the water so that it soaks in around the roots, giving each plant only as much water as it needs.

Gather Water

For most of my gardening life, I've lived in places where water is in short supply, making capturing rainwater for irrigating my plants a necessity. Watering restrictions for gardens in many municipalities can also make it essential.

Collect it: By placing large containers below all the downspouts on your house, you can supplement tap water by collecting rainwater from roof runoff. I use an old galvanized livestock-watering tank, left over from my sheep-farming days, and two enormous steel cans. Vessels like these are often available from hardware or animal-feed stores. Unless you are planning to drink the water, I see no point in investing in rainwater collection systems with lids and filters—the plants won't mind dead insects, decaying leaves or soil sediment. And with a thirsty vegetable garden to irrigate, the water you collect won't stand around long enough to give mosquitoes a chance to lay eggs in it or for larvae to hatch in it.

Channel it: Design your landscape so that swales (shallow trenches) divert water from higher elevations of your garden to where you need it in lower areas. You can also locate your thirstiest plants next to downspouts for easy irrigation.

Keeping the Water Flowing

Northern gardeners and farmers depend on snow cover to hydrate the soil for the growing season. While the top layer of soil may dry out, deep down, all that water from the melted snowpack has collected for your plants. Plants with deep roots, such as perennials, especially trees, pump up the water, helping to bring moisture closer to the surface.

The water that runs off the roof of my house is collected in these containers and used for watering the garden.

Use Mulch to Retain Moisture

Slowing down water evaporation by mulching your soil means plants can be watered less frequently:

Living Mulch: Choose shallow-rooted plants that spread quickly, covering the bare soil. Nasturtiums, basil, savory, marjoram, gem marigolds, thyme and baby lettuce or greens work well. (See Underplanting—Unlike Underwear, You Want to See It, page 48, for more on living mulch.)

Dead Mulch: Good non-living mulch materials include straw, leaves and bark mulch. But be careful—unlike a living mulch that breathes and lets in air and water, decomposing dead mulch can become compacted, cutting off circulation to the soil. Or it can dry out, making the soil unbearably hot, or get too wet. The best non-living mulch remains light and fluffy, so that air and water can easily pass through, keeping the soil alive.

Improve Your Soil's Ability to Absorb Water

Humus improves soil structure, enhancing its ability to absorb water and nourish your plants. Renew the humus in your garden every year by:

1. Leaving the remains of plants in the garden for microbes and soil organisms to break down.
2. Adding compost or rotted manure annually.

Eliminate Bare Soil

Plant your vegetables, herbs and flowers close together, and spread mulch or under-plant in the spaces between them. When soil is covered by a dense plant canopy, water evaporation is greatly decreased.

Water Wisely

As they generally have shorter root systems, annuals need more water than perennials to stay hydrated. And all newly planted annuals and perennials need more watering than established plants. Encourage all your plants to grow deeper roots by soaking the soil around them—even annuals grow lengthier roots with thorough drenching instead of frequent scanty sprinklings. Plants forced to grow their roots to a greater depth need less watering from you, because they have the resources to seek out deeper pockets of water for themselves.

> **Potted Plants get Thirstier**
>
> *Plants growing in pots that live outdoors dry out fast in the summer sunshine—some may even need to be watered twice daily. Hanging pots, smaller pots and clay pots dry out the fastest and require the most frequent watering.*
>
> *Check all pots regularly for dryness by poking your finger into the soil: if damp, don't water yet; wait until it feels dry. If the soil is parched and the plant droopy with flaccid stems and leaves, it needs immediate drenching. Sink the entire pot into a tub of water—a rain barrel works great—for a couple of hours. Remove the pot once the plant has rehydrated and the soil nicely soaked.*

Watering the Vegetable Garden

I water only the soil around the plant roots until it is wet to the depth of my knuckles. Hot, dry, windy weather desiccates the soil, so rehydrating it properly may take two to three hours. Ideally, if you mulch and water deeply, you should only have to irrigate the vegetable garden about once a week. Water the garden in the early morning, before the heat of the day, so plants can absorb the water before the sun evaporates it.

Watering Spring-Blooming Perennials

Asparagus, rhubarb, sorrel, chives and lovage are comfortable in cool weather and start growing before the ice and snow have completely melted away. Like northern humans, they wilt and sulk in hot neon sunlight. Rather than breaking your back trying to satisfy their demands for more water, ignore them—if you let them go dormant, they will perk up and start growing again in late August when the weather cools.

Planting and Watering New Perennial Vegetables, Shrubs and Trees

When planting, loosen the roots, spreading them out to help the plant adapt quicker to its new spacious home. Fill the planting hole with water, and then lower the plant into the hole, letting the roots soak up the water. Next, backfill with soil, tamping it down around the roots. Apply 2.5 cm (1 in) or more of compost or well-rotted manure around the plant. Water the plant again. The compost or manure encourages soil-organism activity, increasing the availability of nutrients, and slows down evaporation, so you don't need to water as often.

Water new plants every week, soaking the area immediately around them, even if it rains. (Obviously, if you have monsoon conditions, don't water again until the soil starts to dry.) Watering deeply and allowing the soil to dry out before waterings teaches plants to grow long roots, helping them become self-sufficient.

After the critical first year, most established perennials need no extra water.

> **Let Plants Go Dormant in Summer Heat**
>
> *Like all northerners, your plants are adapted to cold. So when the temperature rises above 20C (68F), humans and plants alike begin to wilt a little. Extremely hot summers are rare in zones 2 and 3 (with the hottest days usually limited to a week or so in July) but when they occur, it's normal for your vegetable plants to look droopy around noon. Don't worry—this sweltering heat is temporary, and your plants will revive by late afternoon as the temperature drops.*

Letting your plants flower and go to seed attracts pollinating bees to your garden.

Insects, Insects Everywhere…What Are They Good For?

Migratory birds make the perilous journey up north every spring to take advantage of billions of mosquitoes, flies and other bugs that fill the warm air like confetti at a wedding. By early June, particularly in my rural area, the air is so thick with biting, sucking insects that I'm forced to wear a sunhat with a veil covering my face, pants tucked into my socks, and a shirt buttoned to the neck, with gloves pulled over the cuffs of my long sleeves.

Despite all the bugs that annoy mammals, garden plants in the north are not plagued by the same number of munching, sucking insects that can overrun gardens farther south. Using the following strategies, you'll further dissuade or delay occasional insect pests from eating your crops.

And it helps too to chill out—holes in the leaves of plants do not affect their taste or nutritional content.

How to Discourage Damaging Insects

- Rotate your crops (see Crop Rotation Won't Make You Dizzy, page 59).
- Build up your soil, keeping it alive and your plants healthier (see A Healthy Start to a Sustainable Garden, page 20).
- Intersperse blocks of the same plant with herbs and flowers, and practise companion planting (see Consider Companion Planting, page 45) to reduce the chance of your whole crop being decimated.
- Protect your plants with a crop cover (see Crop Covers, page 39).
- Introduce ladybugs and parasitic wasps into specific areas, like the inside of a greenhouse where aphids or other plant eaters have moved in. But remember: if there are no insects for them to eat, the beneficial bugs will fly away in search of food.
- Encourage insect-eating toads, spiders and ground beetles to take up residence in your garden. Provide them with places to live: overturned plant pots and piles of leaves, branches or other garden litter. Give them a shallow drinking source, such as a saucer of water or gradual slope leading to a stream or pond, man-made or natural.
- Where you had insect problems in the previous growing season, spray dormant oil on your woody shrubs and trees in early spring, before they leaf out and when all danger of frost has passed. This kills bugs (and eggs) that have overwintered on trunks and branches.
- Plant herbs and flowers and allow helpful weeds (see Weeds, a.k.a. Wrong Plant in the Wrong Place, page 76) to grow and flower around your crop to attract wasps, ladybugs and other predators.

Insect Pests to Know

These are the pests you are most likely to encounter in your cold-climate garden. Nevertheless, if you encourage beneficial weeds to grow and practise crop rotation and companion planting, you may never see them.

Carrot Rust Fly (*Psila rosae*): Tiny black flies with yellow heads and legs lay eggs in the crowns of carrot, celery, parsnip and parsley. The eggs hatch into white maggots 8 mm 1/3 in) long, which tunnel through the roots. Their pupae overwinter in the soil. It can take up to 7 years to eradicate carrot rust fly from an area, so plant carrots and other affected crops in a new location and protect them with a crop cover as soon as you plant seeds, tucking edges well into the soil or securing them by laying down a 2×4 board. This prevents the fly from laying eggs on susceptible plants. Planting a couple of weeks later than usual helps too—early plantings are most liable to be infested by carrot rust fly.

Tent Caterpillar (*Malacosoma* spp.): Populations of tent caterpillars, black with iridescent blue-white or yellow markings, come and go in cycles and you can drive yourself crazy trying to eradicate them. They won't affect the health of a tree, although you may have to forgo its fruit for the year, since they eat flower buds as well as leaves.

If you wish, you can handpick tent caterpillars off your plants and stomp on them. For bigger infestations, try wrapping the base of the trunk with cloth smeared in a thick, sticky substance, like molasses or Tanglefoot, a nontoxic sticky substance specifically made for this purpose. If your infestation is *huge*, watch out for the bridge effect: as more and more caterpillars get stuck, they form a "bridge" for other caterpillars to crawl over. Obviously, you'll want to rip off the cloth encrusted with sticky stuff (and caterpillars) to replace it with a new one before this happens.

Fighting back against caterpillars can start to feel like a full-time job, especially if you have lots of fruit trees and shrubs. One summer, when the tent caterpillar population was at its peak, I decided the best course of action was to simply escape, so I left on vacation, leaving the problem with parasitic wasps and other predators to work on while I was away.

Aphid (*Aphis* spp.): Common in the garden, aphids of many different colours suck their way up and down your plants like an army of miniature vampires. If the infestation is small, wipe them off with a damp cloth. Or, as aphids tend to cluster onto new growth, snip it off to effectively get rid of them. Your plant will thank you by producing more leaves and flowers.

Attract ladybugs, assassin bugs and other aphid-eating predators by interspersing your crops with flowers and herbs that attract them, and allow helpful weeds to grow (see Consider Companion Planting, page 45, and Weeds, a.k.a. Wrong Plant in the Wrong Place, page 76).

It's a rare garden that contains no aphids—remember that healthy plants can withstand a few sucking visitors now and then; besides, it won't be long before predators fly in to help keep the burgeoning population under control.

Cabbage Moth (*Pieris rapae*): Following a fluttery visit and some egg-laying by the light-coloured cabbage moth, velvety, pale-green, yellow-striped larvae hatch and chew huge holes in the leaves of brassicas, including cabbage, broccoli, Brussels sprouts, kale, turnip, cauliflower and mustard. Use a crop cover to keep moths from laying eggs, setting it in place as soon as you plant seeds or seedlings.

As various stingless Trichogramma wasps are predators, plant flowers and herbs or leave weeds to attract them (see Consider Companion Planting, page 45, and Weeds, a.k.a. Wrong Plant in the Wrong Place, page 76).

Cutworm (*Noctuidae* spp.): You will notice the presence of cutworms by the piles of chopped-off stems lying on the soil. The greyish-brown larvae, 2.5–5 cm (1–2 in) long, live in the top inch of soil, following the nighttime soil egg-laying of adult moths. Protect new seedlings with collars made from toilet-paper rolls, pop-bottle rings, whatever you can find that works, sinking the ring at least 5 cm (2 in) into the ground. As with the cabbage moth, attract Trichogramma wasps to help keep this pest under control.

Northern Slug (*Mollusca*): These tiny slugs (no bigger than your thumbnail) come out at night, so if you are bothered by the holes they eat in the leaves of your plants, head out with a flashlight to pick them off by hand and stomp on them. Or get used to these (harmless) holes in your plants.

Mammals that Ransack the Garden

Dogs, cats and hares are the common big pests in my northern garden, and once in a while we get bothered by bears and on even rarer occasions by moose. This is because I live in the country; if you live in town, the chances of seeing a bear or a moose in your garden are slim.

When bears wake up, they are hungry and will take out bird feeders and eat the compost. I've learned to hang bird feeders out of their reach and empty the light-weight compost bin before their hibernation ends. I've never had any problems with bears eating anything else in my garden.

I've seen a moose in my garden only once. The dogs barked their hearts out but the moose ignored them while taking its time eating the new shoots off willows, their favourite food. If you are lucky enough to see a moose, don't forget to take a photo.

Domestic Troubles

For the most part, bad-mannered dogs and cats are the worst offenders, but most pet-owners will understand if you ask them to take steps to prevent their dog from digging up your garden. My dogs loved to dig in the garden, uprooting perennials and making a mess of my freshly planted seed beds. I solved the problem by erecting a makeshift "electric fence" around it. The fence wasn't actually electrically charged, but they thought it was, as I used plastic stakes and string from my portable electric-fence equipment that previously enclosed temporary grazing areas for my sheep. Recalling some nasty experiences with that fencing, my dogs stayed away from it.

Cats like to use the garden as their toilet: discourage this by planting crops close together and underplanting everything with low-growing ground covers—eliminate the dry, sandy, exposed soil they love.

Hare-y Problems

Common in my rural area, snowshoe hares (*Lepus americanus*) were content to eat my clover lawn until they recently discovered and ruined my kale crop. I've decided temporary fencing, made from chicken wire (which lets in light) is the answer. Using fence posts made from rebar to keep it in place, I can easily adjust it if I increase the garden space. I erect this fencing after I plant the seeds and take it down before the ground freezes so that it isn't damaged by heavy snow.

Plants Get Sick Too

Keep your plants healthy by watering deeply and infrequently. Plant a variety of veg-etables, herbs, flowers and weeds to attract a diverse population of insects and soil organisms. Practice crop rotation to discourage pests and diseases, and encourage a healthy soil community by building garden soil.

By following my own advice, the only plant diseases I have noticed are the two listed below. And I don't have them anymore.

Blossom End Rot

This affects peppers, cucumbers and tomatoes: the bottom of the fruit starts to rot before it matures. Feed plants calcium to prevent blossom end rot. Scatter broken eggshells on the soil around them, and water them with any milk that has gone off and needs to be thrown away (using it undiluted or thinning it in your watering can). Water plants deeply and consistently—if you wait too long between waterings, the dry conditions may weaken them and trigger the disease.

Damping Off

This mould affects very young seedlings, usually those you have sprouted from seed. Keep it at bay by only watering your seeds or seedlings after the top of the soil has dried out. For the most part, if you use sterilized potting soil, it won't be a problem.

Weeds, a.k.a. Wrong Plant in the Wrong Place

Bare soil dries out, is burnt by the sun, blown around by the wind and washed away by rain and snowmelt. These are terrible living conditions for the vital soil communities that plants and ultimately we humans depend on for survival.

Weeds act like a ground cover, protecting bare soil, anchoring it down, holding moisture in and encouraging soil communities to thrive. As covering up unprotected soil is their number-one priority, weeds grow fast and are prolific colonizers.

Weeds fall into two categories: those like dandelions and clover provide nourishment for humans and livestock; others like hawkweed (*Hieracium avrantiacum*) and buttercup (*Ranunculus*) have no food value for either. Livestock leave weeds like these standing in the fields—it is for this reason that weeds in the latter category are considered invasive.

Natural plants, a.k.a. weeds, are hardy opportunists, often better at attracting helpful insects, colonizing soil and collecting nutrients than domestic plants. Take advantage of their free services.

Still, all these plants have some value; different weeds have different jobs:

• Dandelions have long taproots that mine the soil for nutrients, which are accumulated in their leaves, stems and flowers. When they die, these nutrients become available in the top layer of soil for other future plants to eat. Dandelions are up and flowering after the snow has melted and before many other plants have even started growing. Their nutritious edible leaves and stems feed grazing animals. Dandelions can feed you too, along with some other weeds (as noted in Dandelions and Other Delicious Weeds, page 58).

• Clover fixes nitrogen in its roots, fertilizing the soil.
• Hawkweed has a network of shallow roots that hold the soil together, preventing it from eroding away.

Accept weeds and recognize their benefits. And enjoy the surprises: one beautiful plant that came into my garden, fairy bells (*Disporum hookeri*), is a herbaceous perennial with nice reddish stems, shiny oval leaves and clusters of tiny, white, bell-shaped flowers. If I had taken the path of complete eradication, I never would have met this lovely, well-behaved plant.

Cultivate Weeds Where You Can

My food garden is a series of raised beds surrounded by a run-amok clover lawn. Weeds have established themselves in areas where clover has died away and I have welcomed many of them into my yard. These plants—including yarrow (*Achillea millefolium*), cinquefoil (*Potentilla*), peavine (*Lathyrus*), clover and dandelion—have many benefits, including attracting bees and other beneficials. By midsummer, my garden is humming with bees and wasps, and teeming with beetles, hummingbirds, butterflies, dragonflies, grasshoppers, worms, flies, mosquitoes, midges and many other small creatures. If one plant or bug species starts to dominate and the scale tips a little, it's easier to rebalance the ecosystem when there is diversity like this in the garden. To date I have not had a major problem with insects destroying the plants I want to eat; sometimes the plant-eating bugs even chew on the weeds rather than my cultivated crops.

Even the so-called weeds are working hard in this garden bed to protect the soil and provide food for both humans and plants.

How to Say No to Weeds

As useful as weeds can be, you don't want them taking over the annual food gardens where you are trying to start seedlings in spring (unless, like dandelions, they are food crops too—and then you may want to invite some to stay). A few simple strategies for planting your annual crops will discourage weeds from moving in where they are not wanted:

Contain Your Crops: Grow your annual food crops in big pots or even larger containers, such as raised beds. It's simpler to control what grows in contained settings and easier to ensure soil is friable and well watered, making it a cinch to pull out unwanted plants. Your plantings will grow better, too, as pots can be moved around to take advantage of sunshine or be protected from adverse weather. Raised planters dry out and warm up faster in the spring, so are ready to plant earlier, and it's simpler to monitor seed for dryness so it sprouts faster.

Know What You're Looking At: Learn to recognize the annual plants you want growing in your garden by their distinct true leaves. This means knowing, when seedlings are small, which ones are weeds and which ones are your edible plants. It's much easier to remove unwanted weeds when they are young and their roots tiny. Also, recognizing what is sprouting helps you to identify welcome volunteers, like cilantro or parsley, so that you can leave them to grow or transplant them to another part of the garden.

Mulch: Annuals grow so fast in northern gardens it is not necessary to use dead mulch to discourage weeds. Instead, use finished compost or rotted manure around your seedlings. Spread it over your beds at least an inch (2.5 cm) thick to smother weed seeds in the soil.

Let Nature Work for You

The greater your plant diversity, the greater your chance of attracting beneficial bugs: Allow weeds to live in some areas of your yard, intersperse your crops with blocks of other crops, and make pathways productive by encouraging native plants, flowers and herbs along their edges.

Edible dandelions and lamb's quarters growing in my garden beds.

Tighten Up and Underplant: Plant your crops close together and underplant to use up excess soil real estate and keep weeds from bidding on that space.

Weed before They Seed: Before their seeds scatter, pull weeds out of planting beds. Remove any seed heads before tossing the rest of the weed into the compost or leaving it on the garden along with finished annuals, as I do in the fall, to decompose and naturally fertilize the soil.

Don't Dig: No matter how much weeding you do, there will be weed seeds lying around underground in a state of dormancy—that is, until you mess with the soil, energetically tilling and turning it over. When you do this, the seeds see the light, germinate, and you have a problem. Obviously, you can't stop digging entirely, but you can rethink the way you garden (see Minimize Tilling and Digging, page 23).

Make More Plants

Some plants readily self-seed or generously spread beyond their allotted space, and in no time you have too many. Others stick to themselves, are subdued and well behaved, and you barely notice them until you want more—and this can be easier than you might think.

Take Divisions

Herbaceous perennials form ever-widening circles of stems. Sometimes the middle of the plant dies away. Some plants make offsets that form separate clumps. Other plants just get bigger.

You can dig up the entire plant, discard the dead woody centre, and break the plant into its separate clumps or use the sharp point of your spade to chop it into pieces. Good candidates for dividing include these hardy perennials: rhubarb, horseradish, asparagus, sorrel, chives, oregano, sage, thyme, lovage and mint.

Big perennials like horseradish may be impossible to dig up without a backhoe. In this instance, use a saw or sharp spade to carve a portion off the main root.

Just Forget About It

*In my garden, horsetail (*Equisetum *ssp.) blindly pushes its green stalks through perennial crowns, outcompetes my clover lawn and infiltrates my vegetable and herb beds. I've tried zillions of recommended ways, chemical and physical, to get rid of it—none work. There are seven species of* Equisetum *noted in MacKinnon, Pojar and Coupé's* Plants of Northern British Columbia. *An ancient plant sometimes called a "living fossil,"* Equisetum *reproduces from spores and any random bit of root—and it's futile to try to extract this extra-long root system from the garden. I'm learning to live with it: nowadays, I snap off the stalks at soil level so that when I look at my garden I can at least pretend it's* Equisetum-*free.*

I'm learning to live with Equisetum… *maybe, eventually, my garden will be mature enough to outcompete it.*

Layer Stems

Plants that creep along the ground, such as strawberries, thyme and mint, reproduce by layering. Where the plant's stems touch the ground, it puts out roots to make another plant. You can encourage this by burying stems in the soil, although strawberries seem to be able to accomplish this feat by themselves. Once the buried stem has put down roots, cut it loose from its parent, and voila.

Collect Seed

Over the years, the open-pollinated seed you collect from your plants becomes adapted to the unique growing conditions of your garden. To ensure your seed is pure, you need to pay attention to the rules of pollination for each plant. The Canadian volunteer organization Seeds of Diversity (*seeds.ca*) sells a great book that describes the basics on seed saving: *How to Save Your Own Seeds: A Handbook for Small-Scale Seed Production*.

Remember that biennials like carrots, beets and parsley need to stay in the ground for a second year if they are to set seed.

Always gather seed from your largest, healthiest, most-productive plants—this ensures you save the best seed possible for a future crop of topmost quality.

Prune for Shape and Productivity

Plants grow better, look better and produce more fruit when pruned.

Pinch and Snip Annual Vegetables, Flowers and Herbs

As a general rule, regularly pinching off new growth on annual herbs and flowers forces them to put out side shoots, resulting in bushy, healthy, attractive plants. Snipping flowers as they fade stops the plants from going to seed, prolonging their lives.

Prune Woody Plants after Winter's Wrath

Winterkill is inevitable and ubiquitous. After the snow is gone, the ground has dried, and the buds on your woody perennials expand and unfurl, you will notice that a certain amount of their wood appears to be dead. If you're impatient, you may well have already pruned this out…but it's best to wait, as that twig or whole branch might simply be slow to rebound. Of course, broken branches cannot be resurrected—chop them off.

Sometimes, after removing unhealthy branches and deadwood, there is not much plant left. But have no fear—the plant will soon sprout entire new stems and grow additional side branches.

Evaluating your plants annually helps you to be aware of how old the shoots are and assists you in deciding when to chop away older non-productive stems. Refer to Tree and Berry Fruits for Cold Climates (beginning on page 132) for plant-specific advice.

CHAPTER 6

Harvest Time

IS IT READY YET? KNOW WHEN THE TIME IS RIPE FOR THE PICKING

*Y*ou can begin eating some crops as soon as they start growing; others need time to mature and ripen. Some plants produce only one crop; others keep on producing as long as you continue to harvest and prevent the plant from going to seed.

Maximize Your Harvest

For crisp and succulent pickings, always harvest crops early in the day when it is cool, or in late afternoon when the heat is diminishing.

Harvest Small

Pick zucchini and beans when they are small—no need to wait, unless you are competing in the mammoth-zucchini event. Zucchini and beans taste better young; and the more you pick, the more the plants produce.

As soon as the root starts to form on carrots, beets, turnips and even radishes, you can start harvesting and eating them—and this works well for thinning crowded rows.

Beans for eating now and later: it's easy to preserve the excess; nasturtiums for edible decoration, salad additions and steeping in vinegar.

Take Thinnings

Leafy greens, carrots, beets, turnips and radishes need to be thinned. As seedlings grow, they require room to mature. Pull out every other plant in your row…or every two plants. Then, as the remaining plants increase in size, pull out every other plant once again. Always eat your thinnings.

Cut and Come Again

Use scissors to cut down leafy greens by a third to keep them continually growing. You can do this even if a plant has bolted—simply snip off seed heads and the plant will respond by growing more leaves.

Pull the newest growth off leafy greens for baby salad greens—I do this all summer, harvesting the older leaves for the freezer.

Left to right: Crunchy carrots ready for pulling. Radishes: crisp, spicy and ready to eat.

Ripe for Picking?

When ripe, tomatoes turn red…or do they? Many heritage varieties are yellow, black, brown or even green when ready for eating. If ripe, a tomato will always feel soft and juicy, no matter what the colour. Carrots are ready for harvest when they push their tops right out of the soil. Potato vines die back when mature. Garlic and onion tops wither and dry up. Winter squash stems—where the fruit meets the vine—shrivel.

Preserve and Conserve: Keeping Food for Winter

In my sheep-rearing days, I was proud to be able to cook whole meals where all the ingredients had been produced by me. Even today, I grow a large enough variety of vegetables and herbs so that during bumper harvest times—July, August and September—the garden satisfies our vegetable needs, and we still have lots left over for winter.

Learning to conserve the excess food we can't eat before it spoils has helped me keep the harvest longer. Some methods are better than others for preserving the flavour along with the food. Some approaches are better suited for specific recipes you may be planning to make in the fall or winter. And some are just easier, if you are simply pressed for time, or have better things to do.

Create a Root Cellar

Root cellars were traditionally dug in the ground, where the temperature is above zero, so food didn't freeze but was cold enough to remain in a dormant state that discouraged rotting or growing. The ideal temperature for a root cellar is in the range of 3–5C (37–41F).

I made a root cellar (or "cold room") in my basement. We sectioned off a corner, built walls around it and added a solid-wood door. To isolate it from heat from the rest of the house, we insulated the walls and ceiling with pink fibreglass. Next, we drilled a hole through an outside wall, inserting a metal pipe like those used for chimneys, so that cold air from the outside filters in to further cool down the room. When the weather gets really cold—around -25C (-13F)—we plug up the pipe with a piece of cloth to prevent the cold-room temperature from dropping below zero. Alternatively, root crops can be stored in a fridge.

Cure It and Make It Better

To reduce humidity and prevent rotting, onions, garlic, beets, turnips, parsnips, carrots, rutabagas and potatoes need to be properly cured prior to storing.

Keep an eye on your vegetables in cold storage—if anything appears to be spoiling, cut out the rotting parts and eat the rest. I don't have much trouble with this because the winter air that cools my cold room is dry, and my basement is heated with a wood stove that also dries the air. Too much humidity speeds up vegetable deterioration.

Root Crops: Pick a warm, sunny day at the end of October, or earlier in zone 2, to harvest root crops. Lay them out in a dry place—I use my deck. Put aside any damaged roots to eat immediately. Periodically, turn the roots, brushing off excess soil so all sides of each root are dry with any loose dirt rubbed off. Sometimes it takes two days to dry root crops; if so, pack them into boxes or bags to bring inside for the night so they are not exposed to frost, dew or unexpected rain. Lay outside again when it is warm and dry.

Drying the skin of root crops keeps them moist inside. At eating time, I use a vegetable brush to get rid of any dirt; I rarely peel my garden-grown produce. Store potatoes, turnips and beets in a plastic bin with the lid loose on top—they need to breathe so as not to become a slimy decomposing mess, but not receive so much air they turn into dried-out caricatures of themselves.

Carrots seem to need more humidity—I store them in plastic bags punched with holes to allow air circulation, and then put each plastic bag inside a paper bag to keep out light.

The first frost has only killed the tops of these tender summer-squash and bean plants.

Drying garlic helps prolong its storage life.

Use frozen garden tomatoes to brighten up winter meals.

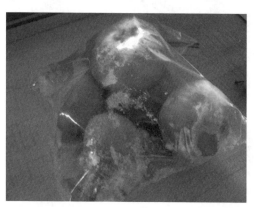

Garlic and Onions: After harvesting, I lay my garlic and onion bulbs on the deck for a few days (bringing them inside every night), until the skins are dry and papery. After brushing off all the dirt, I store them in wicker baskets on the top shelf of the cold room, which is warmer and drier than the floor below.

Fermenting Food

Aussies have Vegemite, the English have Marmite, Koreans enjoy kimchi, Japanese eat miso and Germans have sauerkraut. When I lived in Malaysia, we enjoyed belacan, a black, fermented shrimp paste, to flavour nasi goreng and other ethnic dishes. At home in Canada, I eat probiotic yogurt and sourdough bread and drink red wine. Fermenting food to preserve it is an ancient technology. Many of today's health experts claim the bacteria present in fermented food helps to keep us healthy and disease free. I've fermented cabbage, hot peppers and herbs, and the appealing sour taste livens up my diet. Fermenting food is an exciting adventure and one worth exploring; for reliable advice on this, read *The Art of Fermentation—An In-Depth Exploration of Essential Concepts and Processes From Around the World* by Sandor Ellix Katz. For fermentation recipes, see pages 162).

Freezing Food

I freeze a lot of food—it's quick, preserves most of the flavour, vitamins and minerals, and keeps food a long time without any fear of rotting:

Herbs: Rinse and chop, pack into freezer bags and freeze.

Tomatoes: Wash, pack into freezer bags and freeze.

Berries: Rinse soft berries like strawberries and raspberries lightly. Spread them on a cookie sheet and freeze them hard before packing them into freezer bags. For berries that keep their shape, like saskatoons and blueberries, rinse and pack into bags, freezing immediately.

Leafy greens, beans and peas: Rinse and then blanch—see the sidebar for details—before packing in plastic bags.

Blanching Vegetables

Blanching preserves flavour—sometimes I've skipped this step but found the flavour didn't hold up as well without it. Use this method to prepare leafy greens, peas and beans for the freezer; there is no need to blanch herbs before freezing:

1. *Wash the vegetables.*
2. *Chop leafy greens and large beans into pieces.*
3. *Bring water to a boil; drop vegetables in pot and boil for a minute, or slightly longer for large pieces of kale and collard greens.*
4. *Drain, using a colander, while rinsing with cold water. Be fast—hot vegetables in the colander are still cooking.*
5. *As soon as the vegetables are cool enough to handle, pack them into freezer bags and freeze immediately.*

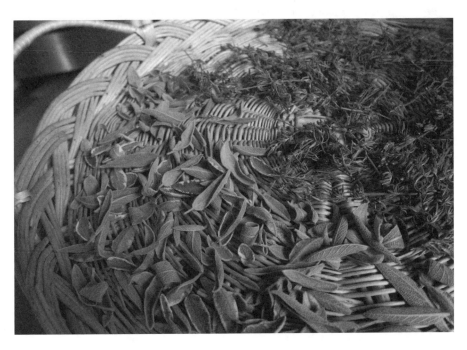

Heat-loving sage and thyme are good herbs to dry.

*Left to right:
Fermented
peppers, dried
mint, oregano
and thyme,
nasturtium
vinegar (see
Flower and Herb
Vinegar, page
145), dried sage
and fermented
green-tomato
salsa.*

Preserving by Drying

The best garden edibles to dry are those that like lots of heat when growing: oregano, sage, thyme, lavender, calendula and tomatoes are good examples.

I lay herbs to be dried on a wicker tray and leave them outside in the sun under the roof gable in case of rain, bringing them indoors when the sun goes down. Within a couple of days, they are dry and crumbly and ready to be packed into jars and stored in a dry cupboard.

Preserving in Oils and Vinegar

I preserve herbs in vinegar or oil as a base for salad dressings, and to flavour my cooking. Herb pestos, especially basil, are made with olive oil and stored in the freezer. See Herb Oils, page 157, and Flower and Herb Vinegar, page 145.

To Can or Not to Can

In my mind, it would be insane to choose to spend a day in a steamy kitchen—juggling boiling water, hot jars and blistering vegetables—when I could be outside enjoying the warmth and sunshine of an all-too-short northern summer. Besides, I don't enjoy eating all the vinegar and salt or sugar that is typically added to canned food to make its taste acceptable after it has been boiled to death. Canning is too much effort for a questionable return. If you want to can your garden produce, get the book *Putting Food By* by Janet Greene, Ruth Hertzberg and Beatrice Vaughan. It contains enough warnings, instructions and lists of what to do and what not to do to make even the most seasoned food preserver shudder.

Storing Food in the Garden

Food keeps best in the garden—as soon as you pick it, your harvest starts losing flavour.

Leave some root crops in the ground for an early-spring harvest. Yes, potatoes, beets, carrots, parsnips, turnips and rutabagas remain crisp despite being frozen and covered in snow for up to seven months. If snow cover is spotty or unreliable, bury the crops with mulch. Prevent it from blowing away by filling plastic garbage bags with crumpled paper, straw or sawdust and placing them over the plants. The point is to keep the plants frozen so they are not thrust out of the ground by capricious winter weather. When the snow has melted and the ground is unfrozen, lift off the bags and harvest delicious, crunchy roots with that unmistakable fresh garden taste. Be sure you dig them all up before they start growing again, sometime in June, unless you are planning to collect seeds.

Hardy greens, mustard, collards and kale stay fresh but not crunchy (which is not any different than if you stored them in the freezer) after the temperature drops below zero. I dig mine out of the snow until it gets too deep and is packed down like the base of a ski hill. Then I know winter has really arrived and there will be no more frigid forays into the garden.

In the north, leave root crops in the ground as long as possible—they keep better surrounded by the cold soil in the garden than they will in even the best root-cellar conditions.

Grow Some Food Indoors in Winter

By the time February arrives, the rest of the world, or so it seems, is planting seeds and gleefully counting spring blossoms. We're counting snowflakes and inventing new ways to enjoy the snow. Sometimes I force an early spring indoors with hardy food bulbs that sprout—including garlic, shallots, chives and onions of all types—giving me access to lots of piquant greens that liven up my winter cooking.

Plant the bulbs in a pot in late fall, keeping them in the cold room. In January, move the pot to a spot in the house where warmth and light will encourage the bulbs to send up green sprouts.

Endnotes

1 Charlotte Gill, Eating Dirt: Deep Forests, Big Timber, and Life with the Tree-Planting Tribe, Greystone Books, 2011, page 81

2 Gaia's Garden: A Guide To Home-Scale Permaculture, Toby Hemenway, pages 83–84

Edibles for Short-Season Gardening

GROW MORE FOOD THAN YOU EVER THOUGHT POSSIBLE

CHAPTER 7

Plan Your Plantings

WHAT TO THINK ABOUT BEFORE YOU PURCHASE OR PLANT ANYTHING

All happy families are like one another; each unhappy family is unhappy in its own way.—Leo Tolstoy

*S*ection Two is arranged by plant family to help you plan your garden using crop rotation. See Crop Rotation Won't Make You Dizzy, page 59, to learn how this keeps your garden healthy by interrupting the life cycles of plant pests and disease. Knowing the plants in each family helps you recognize their similarities, including the diseases and pests they attract and the growing conditions they require.

Why Botanical Names Are Necessary (and Fun)

I love getting geeky about my obsessions. Learning botanical plant names and using them is fun and necessary for accurate plant identification. Plants can have many common names—some similar or even identical to those of other plants—so it can get very confusing. Botanical names, on the other hand, are unique and specific to each plant. They are always binomial (two words): think of botanical nomenclature as a backwards human name, where the first is like your last name and the second like your first. The first name (called the genus, and always capitalized and in italic type) identifies a group of plants with similar characteristics; the second (specific epithet, always lower case and italic) identifies a unique characteristic of the plant. For example, tomatoes belong to the genus *Lycopersicon*; while the second name *esculentum* means edible and identifies it from the other species of *Lycopersicon*.

Lastly, cultivars are plants that have been cultivated and do not occur naturally. Capitalized, non-italic and wrapped in single quotation marks, cultivar names follow the species name, as in *Lycopersicon esculentum* 'Mortgage Lifter' for this vigorous tomato cultivar.

Botanical names give you clues to a plant's growth habit, scent, flowers and sometimes even to the person who discovered it. As scientists learn more about each plant, they sometimes find it necessary to reclassify it and change its name. Often there is much disagreement about plant names and their place in the taxonomic hierarchy; therefore, I've noted the key names associated with each plant. Like anything worth doing in life, taxonomy is dynamic, unpredictable and exciting.

Where to Buy Plants and Seeds

Plants sold by your local nurseries, hardware stores and community sales should be hardy for your area. Plants sold in mail-order catalogues may not be. Pay attention to zone recommendations and realize that they may not always be correct. Even zone recommendations in books may be overly conservative; use them as a guide only. If your neighbour is successfully growing the plant you have in mind, then it is hardy.

Seed Viability

When I first started gardening, I planted every seed in the packet. As I gained experience and confidence, I bought more varieties of the same vegetable, starting only some of the seed of each and saving the rest for next year. It worked great until some of the seeds I had kept for several years refused to germinate.

I discovered they had passed their best-before date. Over time, seeds lose their ability to germinate. Most can be counted on to continue germinating for about five years. Tomato seeds last, on average, a full decade. For the most part, I use my seed within two to three years.

The best way to ensure your seed stays viable is to keep it in a cool, dry place. I store it in the paper packet it comes in, or put seed I collect from my garden plants in labelled paper envelopes. All seed packets are stored in a wooden box in my cold room.

The book *How to Save Your Own Seeds: A Handbook for Small-Scale Seed Production*, produced by Seeds of Diversity, recommends storing seeds in airtight containers, such as a jar with a screw-on lid, in the freezer or fridge. It claims seeds kept like this last many years. Great advice.

If seeds are not sprouting, viability may not be the reason, especially if you are keeping the seed cool and dry. In northern gardens, lack of heat is the main culprit for seeds like dill, zucchini and other warm-weather crops not germinating (see How to Plant (page 59).

I have included two maps, courtesy of Agriculture Canada, indicating first and last frost dates for various areas in Canada. Frost dates are useful in helping you to determine when to plant. See colour insert after page 64 for frost dates and zone maps.

In northern gardens, tender perennials, which wither and die at the first whisper of frost, are often grown as annuals.

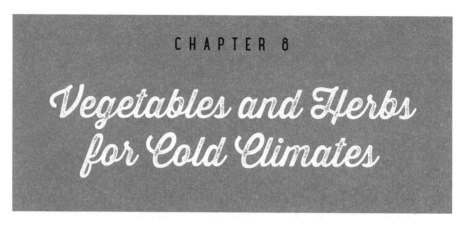

CHAPTER 8

Vegetables and Herbs for Cold Climates

PERENNIAL AND ANNUAL PICKS FOR GUARANTEED HARVEST YEAR AFTER YEAR

Amaranthaceae (Chenopodiaceae)

Plants in this family have succulent, thick, fleshy leaves and stems. They need a steady supply of water for best vegetative growth.

Swiss chard cultivar 'Bright Lights' has stunning colour and tastes good too.

BEETS AND SWISS CARD: *Beta vulgaris* (biennial)

Beta vulgaris has green leaves with red, yellow or white ribs. This unique species has two forms: beets cultivated for edible roots and leaves, and chard cultivated for leaves only.

In the Garden

Plant beet seeds 10 cm (4 in) apart in spring as soon as soil can be worked. Choose an area where soil is light and sandy, not too rich, to encourage big root development.

'Chioggia' produces a 5-cm (2-in) round red-and-white root. Slice the root in half to see its alternating red and white circles that remind me of the inside of a tree trunk. 'Winter Keeper' (also called 'Lutz Green Leaf') produces deep-red roots up to 15 cm (6 in) in diameter. 'Touchstone Gold' has golden-yellow roots with that same fabulous beet taste.

Plant Swiss chard seeds in the garden as soon as the soil can be worked in the spring. Seed tightly for a cut-and-come-again crop (see Cut-and-Come-Again Leafy Greens, page 81) or space plants 5 cm (2 in) apart. Chards like a heavier, richer soil than beets. Fertilize with compost after the leaves start growing—a layer of compost keeps the soil moist, which they prefer. Cultivars to grow include: 'Bright Lights', with red stems and dark-red leaves, 'Bright Yellow' with yellow stems and green leaves, and 'Rhubarb' with red stems and purple-green leaves.

'Touchstone Gold' and 'Chioggia' beets.

In the Kitchen

The leaves of both forms are delicious raw as baby greens in salads. Steam or stir-fry larger leaves. Grate beetroots to eat raw in salads or halve, brush with olive oil and roast on the barbecue or in the oven.

Harvesting and Preserving

Beetroots taste best when they are 6–7.5 cm (2½–3 in) across. Dig roots in late fall before the ground freezes. Lay in the sunshine to dry and then store loosely in plastic bags in the root cellar or cold room. Leave a portion of the crop in the ground for another harvest next spring. See Storing Food in the Garden, page 86.

Harvest leaves continually all season until a heavy frost kills them. Chop mature leaves and freeze—see Blanching Vegetables (page 85).

SPINACH: *Spinacia oleracea* (annual)

Spinach sometimes self-seeds but not reliably enough to count on it. Raw spinach leaves have a nutty satisfying taste that I like in a salad, and contain high levels of iron and calcium, making them a valuable addition to your diet.

In the Garden

Spinach is notorious for bolting. Slow-bolting varieties are available but I've never tried them, as other gardeners say they don't live up to their name. Sow seeds directly in the garden as soon as the soil can be worked in the spring. Plant on the north side of taller plants, like peas or beans, to shade them and slow down bolting. Plant seeds closely to harvest by the cut-and-come-again method (see Cut-and-Come-Again

Leafy Greens, page 81). This also slows the plants' tendency to bolt. For mature leaves, plant seeds 10 cm (4 in) apart.

I grow 'Bloomsdale'—it has lovely crinkly leaves that are succulent and crisp, making it worth the effort to grow them.

In the Kitchen
Eat leaves fresh in a salad as baby greens or cut stems off larger leaves. Steam gently to serve as a side dish or make traditional Greek spanakopita.

Harvesting and Preserving
Chop large leaves and stems, blanch and freeze (see Blanching Vegetables, page 85).

Amaryllidaceae (Alliaceae)
Known for their pungent smell and taste, plants in the onion family grow from bulbs. They like full sun and do best in light, well-drained soil.

Chives are the first plants to start growing once the snow melts.

CHIVES: *Allium schoenoprasum* (perennial)
Spiky green-leaved chives are one of the first plants to poke out of the ground in the spring garden.

In the Garden
Ask a friend for a division of their chive plant or buy a seedling from a nursery. Plant in a sunny, warm spot where the snow melts first for the earliest harvest. Cut off the purple flower heads to keep narrow stalks succulent and prolong the harvest of this herbaceous perennial.

In the Kitchen
After a long winter, chives are a welcome addition to my cooking. I scatter chopped leaves and purple or white flowers on top of soups, salads, egg dishes, casseroles, stews, barbecued meats and vegetables for that fresh green onion flavour and vibrant green and purple colours.

Harvesting
Enjoy chives fresh until July, when the heat does them in. They may start growing again in late August once the days get cooler. Pot up a plant before winter, giving it a rest in the cold room. In January, move it to a sunny windowsill where it will soon start growing.

GARLIC: *Allium sativum* (annual, biennial or perennial)
Garlic does not fit the traditional annual, biennial or perennial label—the cloves are planted in late summer or early fall for harvest the following year. Sometimes I leave

mine in the ground an additional year to grow bigger. Bulbils (the seeds that form on a hardneck flower stem) are planted in fall or early spring and take two years or more to grow into full-sized multi-clove bulbs.

In the Garden

Plant garlic like you would any hardy bulb, from late August through September in zone 2 and from September into early October in zone 3. Buy bulbs from a seed company or garden centre. Don't waste time sowing the stuff from the supermarket; it may grow but you won't get the expected harvest of big multiple-clove bulbs. Choose hardneck varieties (*Allium sativum* var. *ophioscorodon*) like 'Russian Red' and 'Music' or softneck varieties (*Allium sativum* var. *sativum*) like 'Purple Softneck'. Softneck types store better, although I have had no problems storing hardneck garlic until it is gone in January. I really need to plant more.

Plant individual garlic cloves in full sun 5–10 cm (2–4 in) apart. Fertilize soil with a mulch of compost or manure.

In the Kitchen

Garlic's flavour becomes milder when cooked. Roast in the oven for a delicious appetizer or snack. Use it to deepen flavour in marinades, mayonnaises, soups and stews.

Harvesting and Preserving

In July, hardnecked varieties put up a curly flower stalk called a "scape." Snip it to eat finely chopped in stir-fries. Meanwhile, by cutting the scape off, you are forcing the plant to focus energy toward bulb growth instead of flower growth. If you leave the scape on the plant, the flower grows rounder and plumper until bursting with garlic bulbils. Plant the bulbils in the fall when you plant cloves. Bulbils take two years to form multiple-clove bulbs.

I've left garlic cloves that did not grow well in the ground for more than a year until they reached what I considered to be a decent size worth picking. Garlic readily adapts to your garden's growing conditions.

Harvest garlic when the tops start to die in August—pull up the bulbs and lay out in a dry, shady place to cure. Brush off excess dirt, pull off dead roots and tops, and store in an open-netted bag or wicker basket in a dry, dark cupboard.

Garlic scapes are delicious eaten in stir-fries—see my recipe on page 152.

ONION: *Allium cepa* (annual, biennial or hardy perennial)

Like garlic, the best-storing varieties of onions do not form flower stalks that develop into bulbils. Onions are divided into three groups: The Aggregatum group is comprised of scallions and spring onions with clusters of small bulbs, grown as annuals. The Cepa group consists of brown, red and white onions with only one bulb and also

Egyption walking onions are hardy perennials that do well in cold zones.

grown as annuals. The Proliferum group has plants with one bulb and clusters of bulbils around the flower stalk.

Egyptian walking onion, a hardy perennial in zones 2 and 3, is in the Proliferum group. Egyptian walking onions have small bulbs that form bulbils at the end of their stalks. The weight of the bulbils bends the stalk over so that they touch the ground and start rooting, hence the name "walking onion." My first Egyptian walking onions came from a friend. Alas, I did not bring them with me when I moved, however I let it be known I was looking for them and, thanks to the generosity of gardeners, was given a few Egyptian walking onion bulbs for my garden.

In the Garden
Plant onions from sets or seed. Sets are small onions planted directly in the garden as soon as the snow melts. Plant 10 cm (4 in) apart. Start seeds indoors in February. Set the seedlings outside at the same time as you plant sets and at the same distance apart. Plant Egyptian walking onions anytime soil can be worked.

In the Kitchen
Eat onions fresh in salads or chop and sauté to add to cooked dishes. Onions also taste wonderful halved and barbecued or roasted on their own, or with vegetables or in barbecued salads (see page 153).

Harvesting and Preserving
Harvest any type of onion anytime to use as scallions—no need to wait for them to mature. Otherwise, harvest when the tops die back in August/September. If they have not died back by late August in zone 2 or early September in zone 3, bend back leaves to concentrate the plant's energy on the bulb.

After harvesting, brush off excess dirt, pull off dead tops and tiny roots, and lay the onions out in a shady spot to cure. Store in a dry spot—a wicker basket or net bag is ideal—or braid together and hang to dry.

Apiaceae (Umbelliferae)

Most plants in this family are aromatic herbs. Their flowers form umbels—a collection of tiny flowerettes, each with its own stalk, that fan out like an umbrella from the top of a branch. These plants are great to add to all your gardens to attract pollinators as well as predator insects.

CARROT: *Daucus carota* (biennial)

Don't bother with so-called baby carrots—the harvest is pathetically small compared to regular carrots that take up the same amount of space and require the identical length of time to mature.

In the Garden

Direct-sow seeds in full sun a week or two after the last frost date in mid-June when the soil is warm. Seeds take a long time to sprout, so don't lose faith. Thin carrots as they grow, leaving plants 1 cm (½ in) apart. Roots vary in colour, from orange to red to cream. Carrot rust fly is a common pest of carrots; see page 73] to learn how to protect your crop.

'Chantenay' carrots grow well in clay soils.

In the Kitchen

Pulling a carrot out of the ground, brushing off the dirt with my bare hands and eating it right there in the garden is one of the many pleasures of summer. I eat carrot thinnings raw all summer long. Brush whole carrots, cutting large ones in half, with olive oil, and roast on the barbecue.

In winter, roast with potatoes and other root vegetables in the oven. Season with dill, cilantro and lovage.

Harvesting and Preserving

Dig carrots out of the ground and pull off the ferny foliage, letting them dry in the sun and brushing off excess soil (see Cure It and Make It Better, page 83). When completely dry, store in the cold room (see page 82) or fridge.

Leave some of your crop in the ground for a succulent harvest next spring—see Storing Food in the Garden (page 86).

> ### The Best Carrot for Clay Soil
>
> *Carrots prefer light, sandy soil, but no worries if your soil is heavier clay. Get 'Chantenay'—especially bred for heavy soil, these carrots grow shorter and fatter than other types. The carrots are 12–15 cm (5–6 in) long and 5 cm (2 in) around at the top, sweet and red-orange in colour.*

CILANTRO/CORIANDER: *Coriandrum sativum* (annual)

Fresh cilantro leaves and stems contain antioxidants, essential oils, minerals and vitamins. The little round brown seeds, called coriander, are eaten whole or ground. Cilantro can be an acquired taste for some but many find it to be delicious.

In the Garden

Direct-sow seeds in full sun around the last frost date at the beginning of June. Plants grow fast and are prone to bolting by mid-July, which is okay if you want the seeds (coriander). If it's the leaves (cilantro) you want, re-sow every two weeks.

Left: Let cilantro flower to attract beneficial insects.

Right: Coriander seeds are useful in the kitchen.

The plant is slender and easy to fit in the garden amongst larger members of the Brassicaceae family, or add between leafy greens. Grow plants 5 cm (2 in) apart.

In the Kitchen
The whole plant is edible—leaves, stems and seeds. Cilantro is eaten fresh or cooked in Asian or Mexican dishes: curries, fried rice, noodle dishes. And it is used to make fresh salsa or pesto that is better than anything you can buy in a jar. Use as a garnish like parsley or to increase the flavour and depth of salads. Coriander seeds are delicious whole or ground in curries and samosas.

Harvesting and Preserving
Chop fresh cilantro leaves and pack into freezer bags to freeze. Collect seeds to dry and use as spice in Asian cooking, whole or ground.

DILL: *Anethum graveolens* (tender perennial grown as an annual)
This plant is a looker and smells like a dream. Plant all over the garden wherever you have space. Its stature of 60–90 cm (2–3 ft), ferny foliage, large yellow flower umbels and brown seed heads are a pleasure to brush up against when watering the garden.

In the Garden
Sow seed indoors in late April. Dill doesn't like having its roots disturbed, so use a peat pot that can be sunk directly into the ground or start in a tiny pot so it becomes rootbound and less susceptible to root disturbance when planting out. Transplant

Left: Plant tender dill seedlings into the garden after the last frost date.

Right: Collect dill seeds to plant next year or use to flavour your food.

outside in full sun after the last frost date in mid-June. Grow plants 10 cm (4 in) apart. Plant dill with leafy greens and carrots.

In the Kitchen
Eat leaves and seeds. Use leaves, known as dillweed, and whole seeds as flavouring in coleslaw, soup and lasagna. Dill and beets have a particular culinary affinity.

Harvesting and Preserving
Snip foliage all summer to eat. Pack fresh leaves in plastic bags and freeze. Collect seeds by picking the entire seed head and letting it dry indoors in a warm, dry place on a plate or in a basket so the seeds don't end up falling to the floor. Store seeds in a dry container in a cupboard.

FENNEL: *Foeniculum vulgare* (perennial grown as an annual)
Fennel plants grow wild in Mediterranean countries. In Asia, a dish of sugar-coated fennel seed is passed around after dinner to help digestion. In my northern garden, I grow bulb fennel as a tasty vegetable.

In the Garden
Ensure you get Florence fennel or finocchio, (*Foeniculum vulgare* var. *dulce*)—the kind that grows into a big bulb. Other varieties of fennel don't grow succulent bulbs, although they do provide anise-scented foliage, so if you are pressed for space or growing in containers, try herb fennel to flavour food. In zone 2 and 3 gardens, you can't count on plants producing the tasty seeds before winter. Start seeds indoors in mid-April; transplant outside in full sun and rich, well-drained soil in early June. Grow plants 30 cm (1 ft) apart.

Eat fennel fresh, adding to salads for deletable crunch.

In the Kitchen
The whole plant is edible. I look forward all summer to when the bulb has grown big—there's no sense in harvesting early. I like to chop bulbs into a late-summer, fall or winter salad, or cut the fresh bulb in half, brush with olive oil and grill on the barbecue.

Harvesting and Preserving
Dig fennel bulbs up before the ground freezes solid. Cut off roots, brush off dirt, and store loosely in plastic bags in the cold room.

LOVAGE: *Levisticum officinalis* (perennial)
This impressive giant of the herb garden is hardy and easy to grow. By late summer, the plant has gone to seed—be sure to cut off seed heads so you are not weeding out hundreds of baby lovage seedlings the following spring.

New spring lovage
looking green and
delicious.

In the Garden

Sow seed indoors in late March. Germinate at room temperature. Lovage grows into a huge plant 60 cm (2 ft) in diameter and 180 cm (6 ft) tall. One plant is probably enough. Transplant outside at the beginning of June. Plant on the north side of the garden, so it doesn't shade smaller plants. Lovage likes moist soil and partial shade. Well-established plants flower and go to seed in late summer. Lovage flowers attract parasitic wasps that feed on many garden pests, including tent caterpillars and cutworms.

In the Kitchen

The entire lovage plant smells strongly of celery; stalks, leaves and root are edible. I use lovage seeds and leaves as a celery substitute to flavour stock, soups and stews—a couple of leaves are all that's needed.

Harvesting and Preserving

Snip leaves all summer to freeze in plastic bags. Hang whole stalks of leaves and seeds to dry in an airy cupboard.

PARSLEY: *Petroselinum crispum* (biennial)

Despite its ubiquitous presence as a garnish, grow parsley. In addition to increasing and enhancing the flavour of food, the plant's distinctive-smelling leaves help with pest control, as its large numbers of flower umbels attract beneficial insects in droves.

In the Garden

Soak seeds in water overnight before planting outside in full sun in mid-June. I plant in a block an inch or two apart (2.5–5 cm) and end up with an enormous patch that looks like one plant. There are two varieties: curly leaf and Italian (or flat leaf). Apart from how they look, I've noticed no difference in taste. Plants go to seed in the second year and do not produce many leaves. Sow seeds every year to ensure an ongoing crop.

Parsley is a biennial
well worth growing.

In the Kitchen

Use parsley to flavour omelettes, soups and stews, and as a traditional garnish for all savoury dishes.

Harvesting and Preserving

Snip leaves to eat all summer. Fill plastic bags with leaves and freeze for flavouring cooked dishes all winter. Dig up whole plants or part of a plant, pot up and grow on a sunny windowsill all winter. Even though some of the foliage dies, plants continue to put out new leaves and provide a fresh harvest all winter. To make the transition to the house easier on the plant and you, sow parsley seeds directly into the pot and sink the pot into the ground, letting it grow all summer. In fall, pull up the pot, wipe off the dirt and bring it inside.

Asparagaceae

Recently, taxonomists have reclassified this family, adding many genera formally classified in the Liliaceae family. The family now encompasses plants as diverse as asparagus and yucca.

ASPARAGUS: *Asparagus officinalis* (perennial)

Like any seed-grown perennial, asparagus takes three years or more before you can start harvesting a crop. It sounds like a long time but, if you do it right, an asparagus bed can provide you with reliable food for years.

In the Garden

Asparagus is available in the spring as crowns or roots in nurseries and catalogues.

I grew my asparagus from seed, soaking the seeds in water overnight before planting them indoors in late February. When the garden dried out in mid-May, I transplanted them outside into a nursery bed because I didn't yet have enough room to accommodate all my 30 asparagus plants in permanent beds.

In the nursery bed, I planted the seedlings 5 cm (2 in) apart and mulched with compost. In the fall, I made their home by sheet mulching an area of lawn in full sun (see What is Sheet Mulching? on page 33). I planted the asparagus crowns 45 cm (18 in) apart and surrounded them with another layer of compost. Rotted manure would be good too.

Plant asparagus crowns as soon as you get them, just like you would one-year seedlings, in permanent beds.

After harvesting, let the ferny plants grow and die back naturally at the end of the season so they can absorb nutrients for next year's harvest.

Fertilize every fall with a fresh layer of compost or rotted manure.

In the Kitchen

Garden-grown asparagus is tender and delicious raw, or gently steamed and topped with a bit of butter and lemon. Stir-fry asparagus or enjoy in Grilled Vegetable Salad (page 153).

Harvesting and Preserving

Asparagus is up and growing after the snow has completely melted away. Start harvesting spears in the spring of their third year. Break the shoots off just below soil level or use a knife. Pick roots sparingly until their fourth year—then and thereafter, you can pick and enjoy as many asparagus shoots as you want every spring.

Asteraceae (Compositae)

Sunflowers, dandelions and daisies are popular examples of this huge family. Their characteristic flowers are similar in shape. The centre of the flower—called a disk—is composed of lots of tiny florets crowded together. Surrounding the disk florets are petals—actually, individual ray flowers—that protect the disk by closing over it in cold or wet weather. Together, the disk and petals are called an inflorescence. The alternate family name Compositae describes how each inflorescence is made up of many tiny flowers. These flowers attract pollinators and predator insects.

CALENDULA: *Calendula officinalis* (annual)

Calendulas have bright daisy-like flowers in shades of orange and yellow. They self-seed readily.

Calendula flower petals look and taste great in food.

In the Garden

Plant seeds directly in the garden in full sun around the last frost date. Leave some seed heads on plants to self-seed next year's flowers. Plants grow about 30 cm (1 ft) high with flowers 4–6 cm (2–3 in) across.

In the Kitchen

Eat only the flowers. Sprinkle the spicy, peppery petals on food as decoration. They lend a yellow colour to dips and soups.

Harvesting and Preserving

Pick flowers all summer to keep them coming. Dry the petals by laying flowers on a screen or plate indoors; as they shrivel up, pull apart to ensure they are fully dry. Store dried petals in an airtight container in a cupboard.

JERUSALEM ARTICHOKE: *Helianthus tuberosus* (perennial)

Despite their common name, these are not artichokes. Also called a sunchoke, Jerusalem artichokes are tubers that grow underground like potatoes.

In the Garden

Plant these knobby brown tubers as soon as the ground can be worked in spring. Plants grow big, up to 3 m (10 ft) high and spread 30 cm (1 ft) or so in every direction. Harvesting all but a couple tubers every year keeps plants smaller.

Choose a permanent spot on the north side of your garden, to prevent shading other plants. Jerusalem artichokes are difficult to eradicate once established. But why would we want to? Their extreme hardiness, huge stature and small sunflower-like flowers (some years, depending on frost dates) make them an imposing, decorative edible to grow in your northern garden.

In the Kitchen
Eat the roots raw, sliced or grated in salads; or roast, mash or boil like potatoes. Use as an ingredient in Caramelized Roasted Vegetables (page 161).

Harvesting and Preserving
Cure like any root crop (see Cure It and Make It Better, page 83), and store in the cold room or root cellar. Leave some in the ground for another harvest next spring, and to propagate next year's crop.

LETTUCE: *Lactuca sativa* (annual)
There are loads of varieties of lettuce: some, like iceberg, form tight heads; others, like butter and cos types, have looser leaves. I like the cos or romaine types best because they are crisper, tastier and hold their shape better. Butter lettuce has a mild sweet flavour and is also worth growing. While lettuce is mostly green, there are red varieties that look nice in a salad bowl.

In northern gardens, Jerusalem artichokes may not flower before frost.

In the Garden
Sow seeds directly in the garden in early June. Lettuce bolts in the heat, so pick a spot were plants will be shaded by later-growing taller plants. Plant lettuce closely for a cut-and-come-again crop (see Cut-and-Come-Again Leafy Greens, page 81), or space 5–10 cm (2–4 in) apart.

In the Kitchen
Baby lettuce is succulent and tasty in mixed salads. Eat larger cos or romaine leaves whole, dipping them into hummus, tzatziki or tapenade, or break into pieces to make classic Caesar salad. Once lettuce has been touched by frost or gone to seed, it tastes bitter; use frosted lettuce to make Radish Bitter-Green Stir-fry (page 149).

Harvesting and Preserving
Wash lettuce in cold water to get rid of bugs and dirt; dry in a salad spinner and put the spinner into the fridge to let the lettuce crisp up before eating.

Cos lettuce is a crisp and tasty treat on hot summer days.

ORANGE AND LEMON GEM MARIGOLD: *Tagetes tenuifolia* (annual)

Marigold's bright flowers are a must-grow in pots in the sunshine. They will even self-seed in pots: plant once and you'll never have to plant again.

In the Garden

Grow in full sun. Sow seeds outside around the last frost date. Perfect as a ground cover, the plant grows into shrubby, spreading little bushes 17.5 cm (7 in) high, with aromatic leaves and flowers that are said to discourage insect pests. Gem marigold flowers are 1 cm (½ in) wide with 5 petals in shades of yellow and orange.

In the Kitchen

Only the citrus-flavoured petals are edible—use as a garnish or salad ingredient.

Harvesting and Preserving

Enjoy gem marigolds fresh.

SHUNGIKU: *Chrysanthemum coronarium* (annual)

Also called garland chrysanthemums, these plants are known as chop-suey greens and eaten in salads and stir-fries.

In the Garden

Start seeds indoors in April, and plant outside after the last frost date in June. The plant grows to 30–60 cm (1–2 ft) with green lacy foliage and numerous daisy-like flowers with yellow centres.

In the Kitchen

Tender young leaves and stems are used in Asian cookery. Steam gently or add to stir-fries, fried rice, noodles and soups.

Shungiku has edible leaves and pretty flowers.

Harvesting and Preserving

Eat shungiku fresh from the garden.

SUNFLOWER: *Helianthus annuus* (annual)

These iconic giants have immense yellow flowers—some varieties have multiple stems and flowers while others have only one.

In the Garden

Plant seeds in full sun in the garden after the last frost date or start indoors in early May. Fertilize with rotted manure and compost. Every year, I am gifted with self-sown plants from seeds that fall out of my bird feeders. The plant grows 150–180 cm (5–6 ft) with characteristic big yellow sunflowers.

In the Kitchen

Add shelled seeds to baked goods, or sprinkle on top of salads.

Sunflower seeds are a favourite food for birds and humans.

Harvesting and Preserving
Bring flower heads inside so birds don't compete for the seed. Once dry, extract the seed and store in airtight containers in a dry place. Roast seeds, still in their shells, in the oven 250 F (120C) for an hour or more until crisp.

TARRAGON: *Artemisia dracunculus* var. *sativa* (perennial)
In my garden, this is a well-behaved shrubby herb that grows slowly, never overstepping its allotted spot.

In the Garden
Be sure to plant French tarragon; other types grow weedier with leaves that don't have the distinct licorice-like taste. True French tarragon is propagated by root division only—get it from a friend or buy a plant. I found this out the hard way, when I planted tarragon seeds in my first garden. This inferior plant infiltrated its neighbours, forcing me to uproot the whole bed to get rid of it.

Put your French tarragon seedling in the garden around the last frost date. The plant grows 60 cm (2 ft) with slender, shiny dark-green leaves. It will overwinter with no problem if mulched and buried in snow (see Use Mulch to Keep Plants Frozen All Winter, page 44).

In the Kitchen
Pop a leaf of fresh tarragon into your mouth and you will experience a brief numbing sensation, but its licorice flavour becomes milder and more subtle with cooking. Use tarragon to flavour sauces for meat and fish, or steep in vinegar to add to salad dressings.

Harvesting and Preserving
Keep a supply of tarragon frozen (see Freezing Food, page 84), or steep in vinegar to keep available for use in the winter kitchen (see Flower and Flavour Picks for Vinegar, page 145). In addition to flavouring dressings, add a splash of tarragon vinegar to soups, casseroles or stews.

Boraginaceae

Plants in this family have soft leaves and fleshy stems that disintegrate quickly when the plant dies. They are useful fodder for the compost heap. Forget-me-nots, comfrey, heliotrope, bluebells and lungwort are popular ornamental varieties from the Boraginaceae family.

Use borage's pretty blue edible flowers rather than the same old boring parsley to garnish food.

BORAGE: *Borago officinalis* (hardy annual)

Big, hairy-stemmed, blue-flowered borage smells and tastes like cucumber.

In the Garden

Borage grows 60 cm (2 ft) high with small flowers that grow in panicles and are a lovely deep shade of blue. By midsummer, the flowers on my borage plants are humming with bees. Plant seeds in spring as soon as the soil warms. Do this once and the plant will self-seed so voraciously you will never have to plant it again. Luckily, seedlings are easy to recognize, so you can transplant them to a different spot if you like. Use borage as a companion plant all over the garden to encourage bees and other beneficials. I usually let mine grow wherever they seed.

In the Kitchen

The whole plant is edible. Use flowers as an edible decoration in salads, dips or drinks, or candy them and add to cakes. Chop the hairy leaves finely to add flavour to salads, dips and sandwiches.

Harvesting and Preserving

Borage is best enjoyed fresh all summer. You can happily eat it every day and then forget about it until next year.

Brassicaceae

This family has only a few species but there are numerous subfamilies, groups and cultivars. Plants are grown for their edible flowers, leaves or roots, as well as for their many healthful properties. Edible plants in this family are hardy, easy to grow and taste great.

ARUGULA: *Eruca sativa* (annual)

Also called rocket, this is one of my favourite veggies and grown for its delicious spicy and nutty flavour.

In the Garden

Extremely disease and bug resistant, arugula grows fast, maturing in about 30–40 days and bolting to seed quickly. Harvest its oblong, indented green leaves by the cut-and-come-again method (see Cut-and-Come-Again Leafy Greens, page 81) to stave off bolting, and/or plant on the north side of taller plants, like peas, bush beans, pole beans and potatoes.

Plant seeds as soon as the ground can be worked in the spring. Space closely to harvest by the cut-and-come-again method; this also slows the plants' tendency to bolt. For mature leaves, plant seeds 10 cm (4 in) apart. Reseed again 2 weeks later for ongoing harvests.

'Slyvetta' wild arugula is grown as a perennial in warmer gardens—I'm still experimenting to see if it comes back in my northern garden. Last year, its narrow leaves did not bolt to seed until summer was almost over. Arugula has no common pests or diseases.

In the Kitchen

Eat leaves fresh in salads or on their own to enjoy unimpeded flavour. Arugula cooks quickly and wilting the green tames its heat. Try throwing a handful on top of a hot pizza with a drizzle of balsamic. Arugula is terrific made into a fresh pesto.

Narrow-leaved 'Slyvetta' arugula is slower to bolt than its bigger-leaved cousins.

Harvesting and Preserving

Enjoy arugula in season, fresh from your garden. Some pleasures just aren't meant to be available all the time.

BROCCOLI, BRUSSELS SPROUTS, CABBAGE, CAULIFLOWER, COLLARD GREENS AND KALE: *Brassica oleracea* (annual)

Broccoli and cauliflower form flower heads usually eaten before maturity, although they are still edible if the plant goes to seed. Purple or green cabbage grows tight heads of layered smooth or curly leaves. Very hardy, Brussels sprouts grow tiny cabbage-like heads between leaf and stem; they taste better after a light frost or two, but won't survive heavy frost. Kale has risen out of obscurity to become the trendiest vegetable of the moment. Both kale and collard greens—loose-leaved plants that grow on woody stems—are hardy, easy to grow, frost resistant, fabulous tasting (I prefer them to spinach and most lettuce) and jammed with nutrients.

In the Garden

Plant seeds outdoors in mid-May to early June. To keep soil moist and provide extra nutrition, mulch with compost or rotted manure after seeds sprout and plants are producing true leaves. Plant seedlings after the last frost date in June. Water plants deeply once a week.

Broccoli, cauliflower, Brussels sprouts and cabbage seeds and seedlings are planted 25–38 cm (10–15 in) apart. Sow kale and collard green seeds close together if you want baby greens and plan to harvest by using the cut-and-come-again method (see Cut-and-Come-Again Leafy Greens, page 81). Place seeds 10 cm (4 in) apart if you want to grow plants to maturity. As they grow, weed them out (eating them) to allow others to grow bigger.

Kale varies in size and colour according to variety. Cultivars of kale to include: 'Dwarf Scotch Curled Blue', 30 cm (1 ft) high with blue-green crinkly leaves, 'Black Tuscan Palm Tree', growing like its name, although in my zone-3 garden it only reaches about 30 cm (1 ft) and does not attain the stature of plants in warmer areas (usually two to three times that). Still, it's well worth including in the garden for its nutritious and vigourous bluish-black leaves with a quilted texture, which shoot out from the stem like fronds of a palm tree. 'Red Russian' kale has lovely purple-veined leaves that add colour to the salad bowl and garden.

Leave plants in the garden on the chance they may come back next year for another season. My neighbour had success with 'Dwarf Scotch Curled Blue' overwintering in the garden and coming back again in the spring. If your snow cover is scant, try mulching to protect plants from the cold—see Use Mulch to Keep Plants Frozen All Winter, page 44) and Storing Food in the Garden, page 86.

Cabbage moths are notorious for laying eggs in your cabbage, broccoli and cauliflower; see Cabbage Moth, page 74, for strategies to protect your brassicas from this pest.

In the Kitchen

Eat brassicas raw in a crudité platter; smaller kale and collard leaves make tasty scoops for dips and salsa. Eat kale and collard greens in salads, cooked in stir-fries and soups. Blanch kale to use as a topping on pizza, and put chopped mature leaves into curries, stews, soups and omelettes. Enjoy brassicas in Northern Gado Gado (page 155), broccoli and cauliflower in Grilled Vegetable Salad (page 153), and try cabbage in Bubble and Squeak (page 172) and Spicy Cabbage Sauté (page 161).

Harvesting and Preserving

Use a knife to cut Brussels sprouts, cabbage, broccoli and cauliflower heads off the

Left: Hardy collard greens and kale keep growing through little frost, dig them out of the snow to eat as long as possible, or use a row cover to make harvest easier..

Right: 'Dwarf Scotch Curled Blue' kale, 'Red Russian' kale and 'Black Tuscan Palm Tree' kale are extremely hardy.

stem. Broccoli plants may go on to produce more flowers on side stems. Harvest kale and collard greens all summer by picking off the outer leaves or using the cut-and-come-again method.

Ferment cabbage into sauerkraut (see "Real" Sauerkraut, page 163). Whole cabbages keep well in the cold room or fridge; no need to cover them unless they are cut (and, if so, wrap in plastic).

Chop Brussels sprouts, cauliflower and broccoli flowerets and stems into bite-sized pieces, blanch, pack into plastic bags and freeze (see Blanching Vegetables, page 85).

Kale and collards should be harvested from the garden as long as possible and also blanched and packed into the freezer for soups and cooked dishes.

HORSERADISH: *Armoracia rusticana* (perennial)

Horseradish is a hardy herbal giant that grows from roots used to make the traditional accompaniment to roast beef.

In the Garden

This enormous plant grows 1.5 m (5 ft) tall and just as wide with lovely glossy dark-green leaves and white flowers. Grow it on the north side of your garden, letting it compete with other goliaths like rhubarb, lovage and comfrey. Horseradish is typically not bothered by bugs.

Get a piece of root from a friend or you may be able to find it for sale at a nursery or plant sale. A farming friend of mine, no longer in need of horseradish, decided to till her garden to eliminate it. The following spring, every tiny bit of tilled root started growing. She spent all summer digging it up. Luckily for me, I scored a couple of the larger pieces for my garden. Unluckily, when I left the BC Peace, I didn't bring it with me.

Harvest horseradish roots to make a spicy sauce to eat with roast beef.

In the Kitchen

Grate the roots and mix into Basic Mayonnaise page 147, sour cream or yogurt to make a sauce to eat with traditional cuts of beef or as a dip with vegetables.

Harvesting and Preserving

Freeze a piece of the root. Freezing keeps it fresh and stops it from rotting in the bottom of the fridge. To use the frozen root, chop or grate bits off the end; there is no need to thaw it first.

MUSTARD GREENS/MIZUNA: *Brassica juncea* **(hardy annual)**
The leaves, flowers and stems of both plants are edible. They have a pleasant, pungent, spicy taste that decreases somewhat when cooked.

In the Garden
Flowering mustard plants remind me of the canola I saw growing in fields around Dawson Creek. The plant has frilly green leaves, tiny yellow flowers and grows at least 30 cm (1 ft) tall. Plant mustard seeds in the garden as soon as the soil can be worked. Space plants 25–30 cm (10–12 in) apart or grow as a cut-and-come-again vegetable (see Cut-and-Come-Again Leafy Greens, page 81). Mizuna grows fast, about 4 weeks to maturity. Plant as early as possible: sow seeds closely or space 10 cm (4 in) apart. Mizuna has delicate, finely cut leaves and grows only a few inches high. Seed again in late August. Both mizuna and mustard are very frost hardy.

In the Kitchen
The spicy leaves of mizuna and mustard add depth to salads. Steam and eat as a vegetable, add to stir-fries and soups, and use as a topping on pizza.

Harvesting and Preserving
As mizuna and mustard are very frost hardy, harvest leaves as long as possible. Like kale and collard greens, they are delicious after heavy frost. Dry seeds to use in curries and other food. Chop leaves, blanch to freeze (see Blanching Vegetables, page 85).

RADISH: *Raphanus sativus* **(annual)**
Radishes grow best in cool, moist soil in early spring when days are shorter. As days get longer and hotter, they bolt to seed; it's worth letting some flower to attract beneficial insects.

In the Garden
This familiar round, crisp and spicy red and white vegetable is a standard in summer salads. It grows fast, maturing in as few as 28 days. The longer you leave radishes in the ground, the hotter they taste. Sow seeds 1–2.5 cm (½–1 in) apart as soon as soil can be worked in spring. Water well to prevent them from becoming woody and unpalatable. All varieties of radish are good to grow in a northern garden. I like 'French Breakfast' for its unique oblong roots and because I appreciate vegetables that are different. 'Purple Plum' grows delicious roots the size of golf balls. I sow radish seed twice before the weather gets too hot and then switch to growing 'Rat's Tail'.

'Rat's Tail' radish is grown for crisp, delicious, spicy, plump seed pods. Sow seeds directly into the garden in July. Plants grow up to 60 cm (2 ft) tall. They soon bolt and the flowers develop into lumpy green seed pods 5–15 cm (2–6 in) in length. No need to reseed—the plants in my garden produce seed heads until the frost kills them.

Any variety of Asian daikon radish is good to grow. These white roots are long and thick like carrots, and while they won't reach their full size in zone 2 and 3, they are still worth growing for their mild crunchy taste. Sow seeds 10–15 cm (4–6 in) apart in early August for harvesting in September until frost kills them.

'French Breakfast' (top) and 'Purple Plum' radishes (lower right) are grown for crunchy roots, while 'Rat's Tail' radish (lower left) is planted for delicious seed pods.

In the Kitchen

Eat root and 'Rat's Tail' radish straight from the garden, in salads and on veggie platters. Daikon tastes great stir-fried or pickled. Enjoy the greens in Radish Bitter-Green Stir-fry (page 149).

Harvesting and Preserving

Pick radishes, and enjoy in season fresh from your garden.

TURNIP, NAPA CABBAGE, PAK CHOI AND CHOY SUM: *Brassica rapa* (annual)

Napa cabbage, pak choi and choy sum are grown for their edible green leaves and stems. Napa cabbage forms a tight head, while pak choi and choy sum have fleshy stems and succulent leaves. Turnips are grown for tasty white roots.

In the Garden

Direct-seed into the garden as soon as the ground can be worked in May, spacing seeds 10 cm (4 in) apart. Mulch with compost or rotted manure after seeds sprout and develop true leaves. Water deeply once a week.

In the Kitchen

Enjoy leaves and stems of napa cabbage, pak choi and choy sum raw or in stir-fries. Boil and mash the roots and greens of turnips or roast the roots in the oven.

Harvesting and Preserving

Cure turnips by laying outdoors until they are dry on the outside and have formed a skin (see Cure It and Make It Better, page 83). Brush off excess dirt and wrap loosely in plastic punched with a few air holes. Store in a cold room or root cellar.

Preserve pak choi and choy sum by chopping, blanching and freezing (see Blanching Vegetables, page 85).

Wrap napa cabbage in plastic and store in the cold room or root cellar.

Eat young turnips raw.

RUTABAGA: *Brassica napus* (annual)

These roots are easily distinguished from turnips by their golden flesh. They tolerate frost better than turnips, tasting even better after a frost.

In the Garden

Plant seeds directly in the garden around the last frost date in June. Space plants 30 cm (1 ft) apart. Most of the large root develops above ground. Plants survive light frost, continuing to grow until the ground freezes.

In the Kitchen

Young rutabaga greens are tasty and nutritious; eat raw in salads or cook like you would any green leafy vegetable. Eat roots boiled, mashed or roasted.

Harvesting and Preserving

Harvest leaves all summer, but be sure to leave some on the plant so it develops a large root. Harvest roots when 15–25 cm (6–10 in) across before the ground freezes in late October/November.

Cucurbitaceae

Plants in this family need lots of heat to produce fruit. Both male and female flowers are present on the same plant. To increase your harvest—as in get more than a handful of fruit—grow these plants in a greenhouse or cold frame or cover with a row cover. For this reason, I rarely grow cucumbers, preferring to let tomatoes and peppers grow in the prized real estate of my greenhouse.

Cucurbitaceae seeds need lots of heat to germinate; best to start them indoors where it is warm. Their sensitive roots do not like to be disturbed, so sow seeds in peat pots or directly into a greenhouse or cold frame.

CUCUMBER: *Cucumis sativus* (annual)

Cucumbers grow into a bush or vine that needs to be supported. They like rich soil and lots of water.

In the Garden

Sow seeds in peat pots in late May, transplanting into the garden after all danger of frost has passed in mid-June. Space plants 15 cm (6 in) apart.

After cucumbers start growing, apply a side dressing of 2.5 cm (1 in) of well-rotted manure or compost around each plant. This provides extra nutrition and helps to keep soil moist. If you have space, let vining types sprawl on the ground so their leaves help to keep the soil moist.

I did this the one and only time I grew cucumbers in my greenhouse. It wasn't until mid-August that I discovered a bumper crop of fruit playing hide and seek beneath its massive leaves. I made them into a sweet relish that lasted a few years.

In the Kitchen

Eat cucumbers in season when they are crunchy and fresh. Slice to add to salads, serve on a vegetable tray with dip. Grate a small amount of cucumber and mix with minced garlic, lemon juice, olive oil and yogurt to make traditional Greek tzatziki.

Harvesting and Preserving

Pick cucumbers frequently, when small, to force the plant to produce more fruit. Pickle or turn into relish.

PUMPKIN, SQUASH AND ZUCCHINI: *Cucurbita pepo* (annual)

Winter squash and pumpkins need hot summers that last an average of 100 days. If you have greenhouse space or a cold frame, then go ahead and grow them. Try the cultivar *Cucurbita pepo* 'Reno', which takes only 70–75 days to ripen.

You have a better chance of harvesting a crop from summer squash. Zucchini and other varieties of summer squash, often called pattypan or scallop, have a thinner skin and mature much faster. They form a bush rather than vine, are oblong or round in shape and have white, green or yellow fruit. For some reason, growing summer squash outside rather than in the greenhouse seems to be harder in zone 3 than zone 2. I credit longer summer days and more sunshine in the BC Peace for my success there.

Zucchini is known for mammoth fruit, although by the time it gets that big most of its taste has been lost.

In the Garden

Start summer squash seeds indoors in peat pots at the beginning of June and transplant outside in mid-June after all danger of frost has passed. Alternatively, direct-seed into a greenhouse or cold frame after the last frost date.

Zucchini and nasturtiums in the late-summer garden.

Start seeds of winter squash in peat pots in early April, transplanting outside after the last frost date.

Trap heat around your garden-grown squash plants by covering them at night with a row cover in late August, when early frosts are expected (see Maximize Your Results, page 36). Frosts that only touch the leaves won't affect the fruit. Successive frosts will eventually kill the plants.

In the Kitchen
Summer squash tastes fabulous eaten raw, barbecued, roasted or fried. The edible flowers can be eaten raw as a decoration or make Stuffed Zucchini Flowers (page 151). Eat winter squash roasted or boiled and made into soup or pies.

Harvesting and Preserving
Pick summer squash when it is small and tastier. Constant picking induces the plant to produce more fruit, best enjoyed fresh. If you are lucky enough to grow winter squash to maturity, pick it when the plants have died back and the skin is too hard to dent with your fingernail.

Fabaceae (Leguminosae)
Except for bush beans, crops in this family need to be staked or grown against a special fence like pea netting strung between stakes. Buy this at the garden centre or hardware store. I use chicken wire to support my peas, fava beans and pole beans. The chicken wire is tied to rebar stakes that I bang into the soil with a sledge hammer—I know it sounds like overkill, but hey, it works. The supplies were free and have travelled with me from my first garden to my second and now to my third.

Before planting, inoculate legumes with nitrogen-fixing bacteria, available from seed companies. Inoculation ensures the correct bacteria for nitrogen fixation is in your soil. Nitrogen fixation increases the amount of nitrogen available to your plants, helping them grow a bigger crop. See Fixating on Nitrogen Fixation (page 27) for how to do this.

FAVA OR BROAD BEAN: *Vicia faba* (annual)
Fava beans or broad beans are hardy—way hardier than snap or string beans. In my garden, the snow takes so long to melt that it is impossible to get beans in the garden early enough to have a decent harvest if I don't start them inside.

In the Garden
Get favas planted early; the minute the snow melts and ground is dry may not be soon enough because the beans take a long time to ripen. Try starting inside in mid-April in peat pods, planting outside when the weather warms up in mid-May or June. The plants need support as they grow; tie to stakes, netting or fencing.

In the Kitchen
Steam or stir-fry fava beans for maximum flavour.

Harvesting and Preserving
Pick the beans when the pods are lumpy and still green. Pod the beans and then remove the soft green casing around each bean—or leave it—I have eaten the green

casing and it tastes fine. Freeze fava beans: see Blanching Vegetables, page 85. If you are lucky, you may be able to grow them until the beans mature and dry on the vine—if that's the case, use like you would any dry bean.

SNAP OR STRING BEANS: *Phaseolus vulgaris* (annual)

I did not eat green beans until I started growing them in my garden. Purple and yellow beans add colour to the table presentation. Bush beans give you a single crop, while pole beans just keep on producing—although in my northern gardens I haven't noticed any difference in production rate. By late August, with the first frosts in the offing, especially in zone 2, bean production is slowing down anyway. Many people in cold climates grow pole beans, as they take longer to mature, inside a greenhouse.

In the Garden

Green beans grow into bushes or vines. Sow directly in the garden in mid-June after the soil warms up. Extend the season with a crop cover or grow beans in a greenhouse or cold frame. Pole beans need support.

Try 'Thibodeau de Comte Beauce', a purple-splotched green-bean heirloom from Quebec. 'Dragon Tongue' is a yellow bush bean with distinctive brown markings.

In the Kitchen

Serve beans raw or lightly blanched (which gets rid of the fuzzy coating) on a crudité platter. Steam or stir-fry until bright green and still crisp; for extra flavour, cook beans with chopped fennel leaves.

Harvesting and Preserving

Pick beans often to extend the harvest. They freeze beautifully. Blanch in boiling water for one minute, pack into freezer bags and freeze.

SNAP AND SNOW PEAS: *Pisum sativum* (annual)

These include the familiar shelling varieties and less familiar edible-pod varieties. Snow peas have a flat edible pod with no pea development. Snap peas have an edible pod and large pea development, making a rounded edible pod. Snap peas are my favourite because there is more to eat. Choose varieties of peas with the word "sugar" in their name for the best taste.

Left: Pole beans and fennel complement each other in the garden and kitchen.

Right: 'Thibodeau de Comte Beauce' beans taste as good as they look.

'Sugar Ann' is a prolific sweet-tasting edible pod variety.

'Carouby de Maussane' is a snow pea with flat edible pods and pink edible flowers. Sugar pea 'Dwarf Grey' has fat edible pods that grow on short 1-m (3-ft) vines, making it a suitable variety to grow in a pot.

In the Garden

Get peas in the garden as early as you can; peas prefer cool weather. Provide support with a pea netting or fence. If you have lots of room, smaller vining types may need no support—let them sprawl on the ground. These varieties are suitable for growing in a container.

In the Kitchen

Eat peas fresh all summer. Snap peas and sugar peas are delicous as crudités with dip. Eat peas when you are outside and need a little something quick to quell the pangs of hunger. Unlike baby carrots and radishes, they won't have any dirt to wash off.

Harvesting and Preserving

Pick peas until fall, when frosts kill them. Picking every few days forces the plant to grow more flowers, prolonging the harvest. Peas are ripe when their pods are plump. Snow peas are ready just as their peas start to swell. Preserve peas by blanching (see Blanching Vegetables, page 85), packing into freezer bags and freezing.

Lamiaceae

Garden plants in this family are perennial herbs and most are extremely hardy, perfect for growing in northern gardens. Instead of allotting them to the traditional "herb bed," plant these throughout your garden. Their sweet-smelling leaves and flowers attract beneficial bees, butterflies and wasps to pollinate your plants and keep invasive, damaging bugs away. It's a joy to taste a leaf here and there and rub my fingers through their aromatic leaves as I work in my garden.

BASIL: *Ocimum basilicum* (annual)

Sweet basil 'Genovese' is the traditional Italian herb. It has a lovely, complex, deep flavour. Thai basil, lemon basil and cinnamon basil taste as their names suggest. Most basil has green leaves but others, like 'Purple Ruffles', have dark-purple leaves, or reddish leaves, like 'Cinnamon' basil.

In the Garden

I sow basil seeds in my greenhouse at the same time I transplant my tomatoes in late May or early June. Basil likes a lot of heat. Grow it in a pot on your south-facing deck, so you can easily move it inside if frost threatens. Or grow basil in a greenhouse or cold frame. Basil is very easy to grow from seed. Pinch off the new growth to encour-

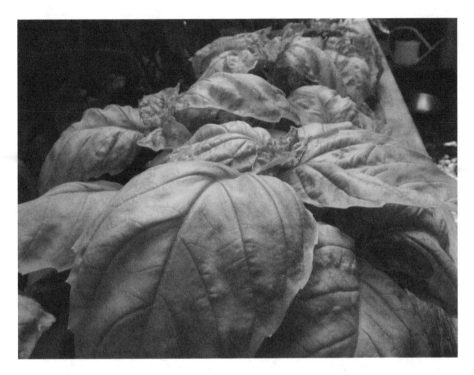

I grow basil in my greenhouse.

age side branching, forcing it to grow shorter and bushier. Eat the leaves you pinch off. Prolong the harvest by continually snipping leaves all summer.

In the Kitchen
Eat fresh in salads, or pair with tomatoes, olive oil, salt and pepper, and eat this combination alone, between slices of bread, or on pizza. Basil perfectly complements any spicy Asian dish, rice, noodles and curries.

Harvesting and Preserving
Age-old garden wisdom insists herbs taste best just before they flower or as the flowers are opening, as this is when the herb oils are at their most concentrated. If this is true, then I have never tasted basil at its best. Summer is not long enough and rarely hot enough to grow it, even in my greenhouse, to the stage where it forms buds, let alone flowers.

Sow seeds in pots in late August to bring indoors to grow in a south-facing window to extend access to this delicious herb. Dried basil has little taste.

Chop basil, mix with olive oil, and freeze; or make pesto sauce, without the cheese, and freeze. I freeze mine in plastic freezer bags, bringing it out of the freezer and using my rolling pin to hack off a piece to slip into winter soups and stews.

LAVENDER: *Lavandula spp.* (perennial)
I use dried lavender to decorate baked goods and as an ingredient in Herbed Salt (page 150).

In the Garden

I got my lavender from a friend. We used a spade to hack the woody root in half. We replanted one half back into her garden and I took the other half home. I planted it in full sun in ordinary garden soil and it's growing well.

Choose 'Hidcote' or 'Munstead' lavender varieties. I've had no luck trying to grow it from seed, and find it's best to buy a seedling or beg a friend for a division or a cutting. Lavender is a woody shrub that survives fine under my garden's deep winter coat of snow. After the snow is gone, I trim it back by about a quarter, and it soon bounces back putting out new growth.

In the Kitchen

Use in herbal teas or fleur de sel. Dry lavender and use to decorate baked goods and candy.

Harvesting and Preserving

Cut lavender flower stalks as the first flowers start to open, and dry in an airy shaded place outdoors.

LEMON BALM: *Melissa officinalis* (perennial)

Lemonade garnished with fresh lemon balm leaves is lovely on a hot day. It's a hardy, sweet-smelling, pretty plant and easy to grow—a must for every northern garden.

In the Garden

Easy to grow from seed, this hardy plant produces lots of crinkly green, lemon-scented leaves. Its roots are less invasive and much easier to remove than mint. Planting it in less fertile soil helps to keep it in check.

In the Kitchen

Brew leaves, dried or fresh, in boiling water for tea. Chop fresh leaves into a salad for a mild tangy lemon flavour. Use as a garnish for food and drinks.

Harvesting and Preserving

Enjoy fresh, or dry leaves in the sun for a winter tea blend. Candy fresh leaves to use as decoration. Store candied or dried leaves in tins or glass jars in a cupboard.

Use dried lemon balm leaves to make a tea.

MARJORAM: *Origanum majorana* (tender perennial grown as annual)

I should grow this delightful herb more often, since its piney flavour with notes of citrus is much nicer than *Origanum vulgare* or oregano.

In the Garden

Sow seeds in pots indoors in April. Transplant to the garden after the last frost date in mid-June. Or grow this tender perennial herb on your deck in a pot to be moved indoors for the winter. Marjoram does not adapt itself to life indoors as readily as rosemary but its lovely taste makes it worth bothering with.

In the Kitchen
Marjoram's sweet piney taste is good for flavouring all winter cooking.

Harvesting and Preserving
Bring indoors in a pot or dry the leaves to use all winter.

MINT: *Mentha* ssp. (perennial)
Mint and its many flavoured varieties need little encouragement to grow. A cutting of mint received from a friend was my first garden plant many years ago, and it has been with me ever since.

   I grow apple mint, chocolate mint (who could resist the name?), peppermint and spearmint. In reality, the different flavours of mint are more about scent than taste.

In the Garden
Mint is propagated from cuttings. Its runners, or underground rhizomes, sprout shoots all along their length,

Any gardener will have no trouble growing mint.

helping it spread throughout your garden. A sharp spade keeps it in check and makes extra plants to give away to friends and new gardeners. Let the runners dry in the sun and turn brown before tossing them onto your compost.

   Plant mint in an out-of-the-way spot or somewhere you don't mind it spreading. The more compost, manure and moisture you provide it with, the faster and more lush it will grow.

In the Kitchen
Brew leaves for tea. Chop fresh or frozen leaves into curries or other highly spiced dishes. Make into a mint chutney or classic mint sauce to serve with lamb.

Harvesting and Preserving
Dried mint is okay for tea but I prefer it fresh. Use mint fresh all summer. In late summer into early fall, harvest it to dry for tea or freeze to add to curries. Strip stalks of their leaves; new mint stalks are tender but older ones become tough and inedible.

OREGANO: *Origanum vulgare* (perennial)
This hardy, traditional, Italian pizza herb is covered in tiny pink flowers in August. Use both flowers and leaves to flavour your food.

In the Garden
This species is easily propagated from seed, or get a division from a friend. It is hardy in my zone-3 garden. Mine grows in a garden bed with a rock wall where it laps up the extra heat reflected off the rocks.

In the Kitchen

Classic flavouring for Italian food.

Harvesting and Preserving

Use fresh or dried or chop into pieces and freeze.

ROSEMARY: *Rosmarinus officinalis* (tender perennial shrub)

Rosemary does so well in a pot indoors that friends of mine decorate their plant with coloured baubles like a tree at Christmastime.

In the Garden

I've grown rosemary successfully from seed started indoors in March and also bought small plants from nurseries, watching them grow into larger shrubs over the years. I grow my rosemary in a pot, moving it outdoors for a summer holiday and back inside the house every winter. At the end of August in zone 2 or in September in zone 3, pay attention to weather forecasts for frost, or check your thermometer, and bring your rosemary plant indoors. In late summer, I just bring mine inside permanently, rather than shifting it about, so I don't need to worry about killing frosts, especially if I'm going to be away.

Like other pot-grown herbs, these shrubby plants have to be watched carefully when brought back inside so they don't dry out, although rosemary is better than other herbs at adjusting to the dryer air and lower light conditions indoors.

Take cuttings from your plant to renew it and make new plants to give to friends.

In the Kitchen

Sprinkle rosemary on pizza, use it to flavour roast meats, roast vegetables or any other oven-baked food.

Harvesting and Preserving

Growing rosemary in a pot is the best way to keep it on hand for use in the winter kitchen. Alternatively, hang stalks to dry in an airy cupboard. Store the dried leaves in tins or jars in a dry, dark cupboard.

SAGE: *Salvia officinalis* (perennial)

Like hot peppers, sage has a warming quality about it that makes the herb a great flavouring for winter dishes.

In the Garden

Grow sage in a warm, sheltered spot. I grow mine in a bed with a rock wall increasing the warmth around it (see Rocks for Heat, page 42). This may be the reason sage comes back in my zone-3 garden. It never survived winter in my zone-2 garden. Sage is easily grown from seed sown indoors in March or April.

In the Kitchen

A classic flavouring for chicken dishes, or for sage and onion stuffing for the Christmas turkey, it's also good with pork.

Harvesting and Preserving

Sage dries well, retaining much of its flavour.

SUMMER SAVORY: *Satureja hortensis* (annual); WINTER SAVORY: *Satureja montana* (perennial)

Summer savory has a distinct peppery flavour. Winter savory's taste is stronger and piney.

In the Garden

Plant seeds of summer savory in pots indoors in early May to transplant into the garden in June. Start winter savory from seed in March or buy a seedling and transplant it outside in June.

In the Kitchen

Use as a classic flavouring for beans, sausages, meats and eggs. Winter savory flavours game and other wild meat, as its stronger taste is more complementary.

Harvesting and Preserving

Dry or freeze summer and winter savory for use in the winter kitchen.

THYME: *Thymus vulgaris* (perennial)

Thymus vulgaris and its many varieties distinguishes itself from the other 300 or so species of these small shrubby plants by being known as the cooking thyme. It is perennial in my zone-3 garden but wasn't in my zone-2 garden.

    Thymus × citriodorus, or lemon thyme, is also useful in the kitchen.

Lemon thyme imparts a slight lemon flavour to food.

In the Garden

Propagate from seed indoors in March. Increase established plants by layering or by division. Grow thyme in a warm, sunny spot. Mine grows in a bed surrounded by a rock wall, and the plants happily sprawl over the rocks, soaking up the heat. I love to brush against them, inhaling their delicious scents.

In the Kitchen

Use thyme to flavour egg dishes, soups, stews and pies. Brew chopped lemon thyme for tea.

Harvesting and Preserving

Dry thyme for use all winter or pot up a small plant to bring indoors. Watch it carefully so it doesn't dry out.

Polygonaceae

Rhubarb and sorrel are the major food crops in this family. Oxalic acid, present in the leaves, lends a sour taste to sorrel; in rhubarb it reaches toxic levels, so only the stems are eaten. The tiny flowers of these plants are borne in large distinctive panicles on tall stems rising above the leaves.

Rhubarb is a perennial stalwart in old farm gardens that have become overrun with weeds.

RHUBARB: *Rheum rhaponticum* (hardy perennial)

Buy rhubarb crowns or get divisions from a friend. I've had my rhubarb plants for years, taking small divisions of the plants with me when I moved. Like asparagus, rhubarb needs to gather strength and grow for three years before you can pick as much as you want. Pull no stalks for the first year and only a few of the fattest stalks the second year. After that, pull as many as you want.

In the Garden

Plant rhubarb crowns 30–120 cm (1–4 ft) apart as soon as you can get into the garden. Mulch crowns with compost or manure.

Leave unwanted stalks and leaves on the plant to die back naturally to strengthen the roots and provide nutrition for next year. This will produce thick, juicy, succulent rhubarb stalks. Rhubarb bolts in July, creating a spectacular display of red stalks, enormous leaves and cream-coloured flowers.

By late July I've stopped watering it, it's stopped growing and I've lost interest in eating it anyway. In fall, I leave the dying-back foliage to protect the crown (see The Sincerest Form of Flattery, page 34).

Rhubarb is pest and disease free. Every garden should have a clump of it.

In the Kitchen

I look forward all winter to my first spring taste of rhubarb's delicious tartness tingling in my mouth. Only the stalks are eaten. Toss the poisonous leaves on the compost heap. My favourite way to eat rhubarb is in a Rhubarb Crumble (page 143) or stewed into a compote to eat with my breakfast oatmeal.

Harvesting and Preserving

Pull rhubarb stalks from the crown, cutting off the leaves. I make sure to chop some rhubarb stalks into a plastic bag, popping them into the freezer, for a midwinter treat.

SORREL: *Rumex scutatus* (hardy perennial)

One of the first edible plants to grow after the snow melts. Even if it wasn't edible I would grow it for the welcome glimpse of green leaves it affords between mounds of melting snow.

In the Garden

Start seed indoors in March. Get plants in the garden as soon as you can. Choose a spot where the snow melts first, such as the south side of a building, so you can harvest as early as possible (see Take Shelter, page 38). Plant other sorrel seedlings in the open garden for a later harvest. Cut off the seed heads to encourage plants to keep putting out fresh new leaves.

In the Kitchen

Sorrel has a distinct sour taste that I love. The first fresh spring leaves have the mildest flavour, and taste great in spring salads (see First Sign of Spring Salad, page 142). Older leaves have a stronger taste that is better in soups and stews. Or use to flavour oils (see Herb Oil, page 157).

Harvesting and Preserving

Harvest leaves fresh all summer. Chop leaves to make a puree and freeze; use it to flavour food all winter.

Harvest baby sorrel leaves for your first spring salad.

Rosaceae

This family comprises up to 3,000 genera encompassing many edible fruit and nut shrubs, trees and herbaceous perennials. Rosaceae is divided into four subfamilies based on fruit and seed characteristics. Flowers of all subfamilies have their petals arranged in a symmetrical cup-like form. Their many stamens protrude above the petals, making them easily accessible for pollinating insects.

ROSE: *Rosa* ssp. (perennial)

Wild roses are common in the north. In my rural gardens I let them grow for their pink June flowers, delicious scent and eye-catching late-summer red hips. Cultivated varieties with bigger flowers in different colours are available.

In the Garden

Plant roses in spring and late summer into fall until the ground is frozen. Hardy roses need little care except spring pruning to cut off winterkill and broken branches, and to keep them in bounds. Fertilize annually with compost and rotted manure.

Hardy roses have exquisite perfume, the best reason to grow them. They come in different heights and shapes, making them useful as ground covers, hedges, vines and specimen plants. Their flowers are single or double in shades of red, pink, yellow and white. Many bloom all summer.

The native prickly wild rose, *Rosa acicularis*, is a valuable free source of food. Find it growing in hedgerows along rural roads and highways.

In the Kitchen

Sprinkle rose petals on food as a colourful, tasty garnish. Candy them and use to decorate desserts. Dry the hips for Rosehip Herbal Tea (page 160).

Harvesting and Preserving

Harvest rose petals just before you want to eat them; unless candied, rose petals do not keep well. Harvest rosehips in fall when they are plump and before frosts reduce them to mush.

Freeze rose petals in ice cubes to float in punches. Keep candied petals in a dry place.

Solanaceae

Plants in this family contain alkaloids that may be toxic. They have been exploited for their medicinal, hallucinogenic and poisonous properties. Because of the plant family's reputation, Europeans were suspicious of tomatoes when they were first introduced.

BELL, CHILI AND SWEET PEPPERS: *Capsicum annuum* (tender perennial)

Peppers can be orange, red, green or yellow, and sweet or spicy. They need a long hot season to ripen. I choose peppers based on how hot they are, and only reserve one or two spots in my greenhouse for them.

Hot peppers I have grown are 'Cayenne', which is hot even when it's green, and 'Aji Pancea', which tastes even better dried.

In the Garden

Start seeds of peppers indoors in March. Plant outside in full sun after all danger of frost, in mid-June. I plant peppers in my greenhouse along with the tomatoes in mid-May. Fertilize with compost or rotted manure at planting time. This is enough as they

Ripening cayenne peppers.

won't flower or set fruit if given too much nitrogen. The more heat and sunshine available, the better the plants produce flowers, set fruit and ripen.

Many pepper plants, sweet and hot, are small enough to grow in containers. This is good news, as at the end of the season pots can be set indoors in a sunny windowsill where their fruit will continue to ripen.

In the Kitchen
Whether you're cooking Mexican or Asian food, hot peppers are a must. Eat sweet peppers raw, roasted in the oven or grilled on the barbecue for that smoky flavour.

Harvesting and Preserving
Peppers ripen in late August to September. They are edible at any stage of growth, but be sure to pick all fruit before frost kills them.

Peppers can be dried or frozen.

Ground cherries grow on short, sprawling plants. Each yellow fruit grows inside a green papery husk.

GROUND CHERRY: *Physalis pruinosa* (annual)
Like tomatillos, these need lots of heat to ripen a crop. However, ground cherries are smaller, so grow them in a pot you can move indoors or on the south side of bigger crops like bush beans, which will shelter them.

In the Garden
The plant grows into a short bush with yellow 2-cm (¾-in) berries. The berries are inside a husk that dries to a papery brown. Sow seeds indoors 6–8 weeks before the last frost date. Transplant seedlings outside about a week or so after the last frost date.

In the Kitchen
Fancy restaurants use ground cherries as decorations for desserts. They have a taste somewhat reminiscent of apples or plums. Eat like you would any berry or make into jam.

Harvesting and Preserving

Berries are ripe when the husk has turned brown and the fruit is burnished yellow-gold in colour. Pull the husk off to eat, but leave it on for storing. Store ground cherries in a single layer in a box or other container in a root cellar, or freeze the husked fresh fruit packed into plastic bags.

POTATO: *Solanum tuberosum* (perennial usually grown as an annual)

There are early, midseason and late varieties of potatoes. Potatoes can be eaten anytime. You don't need to wait for them to mature, although I've avoided planting potatoes labelled "late season." I love 'Purple Viking', a waxy variety that has blue skin and white flesh and is nice baked or boiled. I also grow a fingerling type that has yellow flesh and skin. Their starchy texture makes them perfect for frying and baking, but they disintegrate if boiled, which is great for potato soup.

In the Garden

Plant potatoes as soon as the soil is workable in spring. Plant whole potatoes or chop into pieces, making sure each piece contains an eye, the spot where the shoots grow. Although the tubers are hardy, the tops will be killed by frost. One year, the tops of my potato crop were killed twice by late spring frosts, but each time the plants revived, regrowing in a few days.

Plant potatoes with the eye facing upward in holes 45 cm (18 in) apart. As they grow, fill in the holes with soil and mulch. Tubers develop above the eyes. Hilling the soil or mulching on top of the eye keeps the developing tubers buried. Tubers exposed to light turn green and may contain the toxin solanine.

In the Kitchen

Waxy potatoes hold their shape and are good for dishes like salads or roasts when you want the potatoes to remain whole.

Starchy potatoes don't hold their shape. Their fluffy texture is absorbent, which is ideal for soaking up butter, sour cream, or oil in a frying pan. They are not good

Potato tops die off and disappear. Mark the spot with a stick where they are planted so you can easily find it come spring for another harvest.

as mashed potatoes because it's easy to overwork them and end up with a tasteless gluey mess.

All-purpose potatoes are in-between and work well in almost any potato dish.

Harvesting and Preserving

When I lived in the Peace my neighbour came over with a box of three varieties of potatoes for my garden: red, yellow and white. They were the extras she had after planting her own crop. Every year she saved potatoes specifically for replanting. Now I do the same. I choose big healthy tubers as my seed for next year's crop.

Dig new potatoes as soon as they have reached a reasonable size, in as little as a month after they start growing.

Potatoes are mature when the tops die down in late August to September. They will store fine in the garden and can be left there over winter for a fresh spring crop. See Storing Food in the Garden, page 86.

Dig potatoes for winter storage on a sunny day in September or October before the ground is frozen. Lay out in the sunshine to cure, turning periodically to make sure they dry (see Cure It and Make It Better, page 83). Brush off excess soil. I pile mine into a plastic box with a lid that I let sit loosely on top. Store potatoes in a root cellar. Monitor periodically, adjusting the lid accordingly as the potatoes adapt to their new home. You don't want the potatoes to get so dry that they start to shrivel; neither do you want them to be so damp that they start rotting.

TOMATILLOS: *Physalis ixocarpa* (annual)

These are a novelty plant in that you probably won't harvest more than a handful of fruit unless you give them space inside your greenhouse. Tomatillos need a long hot season.

In the Garden

Plants grow into bushes about 1 m (3 ft) tall. The green fruit grows in a green, papery husk. Sow seeds 6–8 weeks before planting outside in the garden or greenhouse. Protect plants with a row cover towards the end of the season.

In the Kitchen

Use to make authentic salsa verde or substitute for any dish requiring green tomatoes.

Harvesting and Preserving

Pick tomatillos when their fruit fills the husks. Pull the husks off the fruit before eating or storing. Tomatillos can be canned or frozen.

TOMATO: *Lycopersicon esculentum* (tender perennial)

Typically, short-season gardeners are reduced to growing tomatoes with the words "arctic," "siberian" or "glacier" in their name, but don't limit yourself. By growing tomatoes from seed, starting them indoors in late March and growing them in a greenhouse, you can grow tomatoes of almost any variety to maturity.

Tomatoes grow as either determinate shrubs producing one crop that ripens at the same time or as indeterminate vines that grow on and on, producing tomatoes that ripen at different times.

There are loads of tomato varieties. Growing open-pollinated or heritage varieties of tomatoes is trendy. The fruit is green, black, brown, purple and yellow, as well as red. They range in size from tiny currant to gigantic fruits bigger than baseballs and can be round, oblong, oval, cylindrical and pear shaped.

Good varieties of determinate tomatoes I have grown include 'Silvery Fir' and 'Starfire'.

Tasty varieties of indeterminate tomatoes are 'Brandy Wine', 'Black Krim', 'Purple Calabash', 'Red Currant', 'Purple Truffle', 'Arbuznyi' and 'Burracker's Favorite'.

Fleshy, thick types like 'Roma' are used to make sauces and are better for drying than thinner juicy types.

The number of varieties and diversity of colour, shape and taste of heirloom tomatoes is staggering.

In the Garden

Pick the hottest, sunniest part of your garden to grow tomatoes, like the south side of a building or wall. Growing tomatoes in a greenhouse, or beneath a cold frame is expected for types that take longer than 65 days to mature. Reserve this prime real estate for those varieties to get the largest, ripest crop possible.

In northern gardens too much heat is usually not a problem. One year, I was slow to open my greenhouse doors and windows. The midday sun was only putting out an average amount of heat but inside the tightly shut greenhouse, this smaller amount of heat was multiplied, increasing the temperature of the greenhouse to fatal proportions and killing many tomato flowers. Dead flowers do not produce fruit. Be sure to open your greenhouse doors and windows on sunny late June, July, August and even some September days.

Start tomato seeds indoors about 6–8 weeks before planting outside in pots, a greenhouse or in the garden. Germinate in a warm spot 21–30C (70–85F). I germinate tomato seeds under lights in March in the basement where the woodstove keeps them warm.

I plant tomatoes in the greenhouse in May when the snow is gone and things are starting to grow outside. My greenhouse is able to fend off light frosts and I use plastic milk jugs full of water, placed next to each plant, to keep them warm in early spring and during cold nights (see Heat Things Up in the Greenhouse, page 41).

Plant tomatoes outside in pots or directly into the ground after all danger of frost has passed in the first week or so of June. Space 45 cm (18 in) apart.

Encourage strong roots by burying seedlings in the soil up to their necks, the first row of true leaves. They'll sprout more roots all along the buried stem.

Water deeply and evenly about once a week to further encourage long roots.

Grow tomatoes with companions like basil, marigold and lettuce to cover up the soil around their stems.

Growing tomatoes in pots

Growing tomatoes in pots makes them more versatile, as you can move them around to take advantage of hot spots in your garden. I grow potted tomatoes against the wall of the house on my south-facing deck.

Choose pots for tomatoes based on their eventual size: grow big indeterminate types in garbage-can sized pots; midsized determinate types in pots with about a 45-cm (18-in) diameter; dwarf varieties in pots that are approximately 25 cm (10 in) in diameter.

In general, pick pots that are deep rather than shallow to accommodate the plants' large root systems.

'Starfire' tomatoes were bred at the Morden experimental farm in Manitoba in 1963. They're a Canadian heirloom. I grow the determinate plant in a pot in the greenhouse, in mid May waiting for the weather to improve so I can bring it outside to the deck on the south side of the house.

Pruning

Pruning the top off indeterminate tomatoes in mid-August to stop them from growing forces them to concentrate on ripening fruit. Pruning the suckers that grow between the stem and side branches also helps concentrate the harvest. Pruning indeterminate tomatoes keeps the plants tidy and manageable.

Most years I don't bother pruning for tidiness. Summer is so short and I want lots of tomatoes, green or red.

In the Kitchen

Eat tomatoes fresh, still warm from the sun, or add them to almost any dish where they support the main ingredient. Let them shine by themselves or drizzled with pesto and use in soups, stews, sauces and salads.

Harvesting and Preserving

Tomatoes are ready when they are soft and juicy and have reached their mature colour. They start ripening in August and continue until the killing frosts of September. Tomatoes can be frozen, dried or canned. Once picked, store at room temperature for best flavour.

When Tomatoes Are Still Green

By late September, nightly frosts with lower and lower temperatures occur every night. At this point, I start to think that what's left of the tomato crop would be better off inside. I might lose a few due to rot but at least the rest of the crop won't be killed by frost.

Ethylene gas, a natural product of ripening fruit, can be used to ripen those green tomatoes. Place tomatoes inside paper bags or boxes in a single layer, along with an apple or pear. Close the bags and set them on the kitchen counter. Check bags daily for ripening tomatoes and any that might be going off.

Drying Tomatoes

Excited by a magazine article on sun-drying tomatoes for delectable flavour, I followed its steps using my heirloom tomatoes, with the disappointing result of just juice and skin. Later, I found out that I should have used 'Roma' or another meaty tomato. Here's how to dry 'Roma' tomatoes:

1. *Cut tomatoes in half and lay on a baking pan.*
2. *Sprinkle with salt to help sweat out the moisture.*
3. *Place in an oven set at 95C (200F), leaving the door slightly ajar to help eliminate moisture—tomatoes will take 4 or more hours to dry, depending on juiciness.*
4. *Tomatoes are ready when dry on the outside and still moist but not juicy on the inside.*
5. *Store in a dry, clean jar in the fridge; they'll stay fresh for a couple of months.*

Tropaeolaceae

Nasturtiums are the best known plant in this family of annual or herbaceous perennial herbs with slightly succulent stems. Their flowers arise on stems between the main stem and a leaf. Flowers are zygomorphic, meaning they can be divided in half and have symmetrical sides.

NASTURTIUM: *Tropaeolum majus* (annual)

Nasturtiums are grown for their intense jewel-coloured flowers, in shades of yellow, red and orange, and round leaves. Some varieties to try are the low-growing 'Alaska' series, with variegated foliage, and the 'Whirlybird' series, with green foliage. The heirloom variety 'Empress of India' has striking red flowers and grows into a vine.

In the Garden

Germinate flowers indoors a week or two before planting outside in full sun, after the last frost date. Plant anywhere in the garden for bright hits of colour. They are known to attract aphids, and this can be helpful as these pests will congregate on the nasturtiums, mostly ignoring the rest of the edibles in the garden.

In the Kitchen

The whole plant is edible. The leaves and flowers have a spicy, peppery taste. Add to salads, or use as a garnish. Be sure to rinse the flowers before eating to get rid of any aphids.

Harvesting and Preserving

Enjoy nasturtiums when they are fresh or steep the flowers in vinegar (see Flower and Herb Vinegar, page 145).

Violaceae

Many species in this family are native to northern BC. Plants can be perennial or voracious self-seeding annuals. *Viola odorata* and hybrids are grown for their exquisite perfume. Violet flowers are highly specialized for insect pollination. This fact alone makes them a must to grow in your sustainable garden.

Nasturtium's bright flowers are one of the first casualties of frost.

VIOLETS: *Viola tricolor* (annual); *Viola cornuta* (perennial)

I got my first viola (or Johnny-jump-up) growing in a spade full of mint from a friend. Since then it has reseeded voraciously, admirably hitching a ride in my potted perennials to my other gardens. I can't imagine a garden without these happy flowers popping up all over the place.

In the Garden

Sow violets from seed or get them from a friend's garden. Plant anywhere: sun, shade, lush garden soil or gravel. Deadhead to prolong flowering. You only need to plant violets once. They'll reseed themselves all over your garden.

In the Kitchen

Use flowers as a garnish in summer drinks, salads and appetizers. Use candied violets to decorate desserts.

Harvesting and Preserving

Candied violets keep a few weeks in a dry container.

I love the happy face of the ubiquitous Johnny-jump-up violet that grows all over my garden.

CHAPTER 9

Tree and Berry Fruits for Cold Climates

THESE ARE THE STANDBYS—WHAT EVERY NORTHERN GARDENER SHOULD GROW

Old farmhouse gardens always contain an apple tree, gnarled with age but still producing sweet fruit; there may be a prickly raspberry patch, suckers popping up everywhere; and strawberries running this way and that. These are the old standbys, the popular fruits every northern gardener should grow.

Fruit trees and bushes do best planted in well-drained soil, in full sun. After planting, fertilize with a layer of compost or well-rotted manure. Water the roots deeply once a week for the first year to help them get established.

Sweet strawberries are a summer treat from my garden.

In succeeding years, fertilize with compost or manure, spreading it right out to the drip line. Plant clover or other nitrogen-fixing plants to cover the ground (see Fixating on Nitrogen Fixation, page 27). Clover's deep roots break up the soil, bring up water from the earth's depths and increase the amount of nitrogen available to your fruit trees and shrubs.

Actinidiaceae

This small family mostly consists of subtropical or tropical, deciduous, woody shrubs or vines. The plants are native to Asia, Australia, and South and Central America. Kiwi fruit is the family's best-known plant. Despite its tropical origins, the kiwi species *Actinidia arguta* is hardy in zone 3 and possibly zone 2.

KIWI: *Actinidia arguta* (perennial)

When I bought my kiwi plant, I was told to get the variety 'Issia', which is self-pollinating. I planted it on the south side of the house, building a trellis to support it. Its tiny fruit have a delicious strawberry taste.

In the Garden

Kiwi grows into a 6-m (20-ft) vine with fragrant white flowers and thumb-sized green fruit. Grow on a trellis. Recent cultivars have both female and male parts, so there is no need to have more than one plant for pollination.

In the Kitchen

Eat kiwi fruit fresh or make into crumbles, pies and coffee cakes.

Harvesting and Preserving

Kiwi fruit ripens in late August. Eat fresh or pile the tiny fruit into freezer bags and freeze.

Caprifoliaceae

Plants in this family are mostly ornamental woody shrubs or vines. Flowers are tubular shaped and often fragrant, and the fruit is usually a berry.

HASKAP: *Lonicera caerulea* (perennial)

Haskap is native to the northern boreal forests of Asia, Europe and North America. Five varieties have been developed at the University of Saskatchewan for Canada: 'Tundra', 'Borealis', 'Aurora', 'Honeybee' and the 'Indigo' series. The flowers can survive temperatures as low as -7C (19F), thus the oblong, blue fruit is ripe and ready to eat as early as June. They are also known as honeyberries or sweet berry.

In the Garden

Haskap shrubs grow 120–150 cm (4–5 ft) high. They are hardy, high yielding, don't sucker, require no pruning and grow fast. Haskap needs another genetically distinct variety for pollination. Plant haskap shrubs 60 cm (2 ft) apart to grow a hedge.

In the Kitchen

Pick haskap berries when they are dark blue, plump and juicy for best taste. If they are picked too early they taste tart, although some people report that some varieties taste tart no matter when you pick them. Process the tart berries the same way you would rhubarb by adding sugar and incorporating them into baking, or make jam. Eat haskap berries fresh too.

Harvesting and Preserving

Process haskap berries into jam (see Freezer Garden Berry Jam, page 169), juice or freeze.

Ericaceae

This family likes acidic soil. Many of its plants are native to northern BC. Wild blueberries and cranberries can be found growing in meadows at low elevations.

BLUEBERRY: *Vaccinium* ssp. (perennial)

You can find native blueberries growing in clearings along the side of the road or in meadows in the bush. Domestic blueberries need a lot of work to maintain the shrubs' productivity. Even though some blueberries are capable of self-pollination, it is better to have more than one cultivar to increase fruit set. Ask your nursery for advice.

In the Garden

Plant in moist acidic soil. Increase soil acidity with pine needles or peat moss. Remove all flower heads for the first two years to encourage root development. Fruit buds are bigger and grow near the tips of the canes and on the tips of lateral shoots. In the third year allow a few buds to flower and set fruit. From the fourth year onward allow plants to set a full crop.

Second- and third-year growth with strong laterals are the best fruiting wood.

Pruning

For maximum harvest, blueberry plants need to be pruned annually. After the fourth year, look for old canes with weak laterals and few flower buds; prune these back to a strong side shoot or prune off at the base. Fruit produced on older canes is smaller and not worth growing. Old canes are thicker with grey peeling bark. Aim to have plants with one or two new canes every year and no canes more than four years old.

In the Kitchen

Eat blueberries fresh or use in baking.

Harvesting and Preserving

Blueberries ripen in July. Make into jam (see Freezer Garden Berry Jam, page 169) or freeze.

Grossulariaceae

These plants are shrubs from temperate regions, with berries as fruit. There are many native species growing in clearings in the bush along the sides of highways and country roads.

CURRANT AND GOOSEBERRY *Ribes* ssp. (perennial)

Black, red and white cultivars of currants are available; the fruit is small and tart, and good varieties to grow are 'Red Lake' and 'Magnus'. Gooseberries have thorns and bigger and juicier black, red, pink or white fruit. 'Pembina Pride' is a gooseberry variety well worth growing.

In the Garden

Some currants need another variety for pollination. In some cases, cross-pollination improves fruit set. Ask your local nursery for advice when buying currant bushes.

Gooseberries are self-pollinating.

Remove flowers from new plants the first year to help roots develop. Allow them to set fruit in the second year. They grow best in cool, moist, clayey soil. *Ribes* will produce fruit even if grown in shade.

Pruning

Prune plants when they are dormant in late April or early May.

Black currants produce their best crop on one-year-old wood. Strong year-old shoots or two- and three-year-old shoots with year-old branches are best. Prune off any shoots older than three years.

Red currants and gooseberries produce their fruit on spurs on two- or three-year-old wood. Prune off any shoots older than three years.

In the Kitchen

Eat currants and gooseberries fresh or use in baking.

Harvesting and Preserving

Freeze, or make currants and gooseberries into wine or jam (see Freezer Garden Berry Jam, page 169).

Rosaceae

Most of our edible fruit and berries are classified in the Rosaceae family. Edible fruit range in habit from low-growing herbs, bushes, shrubs and trees. The unifying feature of this family is their similar arrangement of reproductive structures, a.k.a. flowers.

APPLES AND CRABAPPLES: *Malus* ssp. (perennial)

There are many varieties, some of which are ornamental and grown only for flowers. To ensure pollination and get fruit, you need to grow at least two different varieties of apples. They can be crabapples, regular apples or ornamental varieties.

Hardy apples have been developed to grow on the Canadian prairies. 'Norland',

'Heyer', 'Goodland', 'Battleford' and 'Dolgo', a crabapple, are some popular types, but there are many more varieties.

In the Garden

Plant trees in full sun. Position the trunk so the graft union, the swollen part of the lower trunk, is 5–10 cm (2–4 in) above the soil line. Fertilize annually with compost and rotted manure.

Pruning *Malus* and *Prunus* Trees

Prune in early spring before trees start growing. Cut off any shoots that are crossing, taking into account lateral and vertical shoot spacing. Thin out twiggy growth. Prune older growth or areas with little growth to stimulate the tree to produce new growth. Overall, prune moderately to maintain a balance between woody growth and fruit production.

In the Kitchen

Eat fresh or use in baking all winter.

Harvesting and Preserving

Depending on variety, apples and crabapples are ready for picking from late August until late September. Store apples in the root cellar. Apples can be easily be made into applesauce.

CHERRY AND PLUM: *Prunus* ssp. (perennial)

Hardy varieties of cherries are *Prunus cerasus* and *P. fruticosa* hybrids. Their fruit is either tart or sour. Look for 'Evans' or North Star'.

Prunus tomentosa (Nanking cherry) is the first shrub to flower in spring, before it leafs out, and is a heavy producer of bright-red cherries.

Prunus virginiana (chokecherry) 'Shubert' has white flowers followed by tiny black cherries. Its green leaves turn burgundy in summer.

Plum trees to look for include *Prunus salicina* and 'Pembina'.

In the Garden

Whether growing trees or shrubs, you need two different varieties of *Prunus* for pollination. Plant in early spring or fall in full sun.

In the Kitchen

Eat fresh or use in baking.

Harvesting and Preserving

Plums and cherries ripen from July onward. For maximum harvest, get to them before the birds do. Process cherries and plums into jam (see Freezer Garden Berry Jam, page 169), juice or freeze.

RASPBERRY: *Rubus* ssp. (biennial or perennial)

Recommended varieties of raspberries to try include 'Boyne', 'Killarney' and the yellow variety 'Honey Queen'.

Raspberry roots are perennial; individual canes are biennial, meaning they take two years to produce fruit.

In the Garden

Plant canes about 30 cm (1 ft) apart in early spring or fall. Bury the crowns 4 cm (1½ in) deep, and mulch with compost or rotted manure. The first year the canes grow leaves, the next they produce fruit. In fall, after the fruit is finished, cut down those canes. New shoots will grow from the base. In spring, after the canes have leafed out, prune out any that are dead and cut off winterkilled tips.

In the Kitchen

The best way to eat raspberries is fresh, but excess fruit freezes well and makes delicious jam (see Freezer Garden Berry Jam, page 169).

Harvesting and Preserving

Raspberries ripen from July onwards. To freeze raspberries lay on a tray or cookie sheet in a single layer and put it in the freezer. When frozen pack into freezer bags.

SASKATOON: *Amelanchier alnifolia* (perennial)

When I lived in the BC Peace, I dug saskatoon shrubs from the bush and transplanted them into my garden. For my new garden I decided it was easier to buy commercial saskatoon varieties.

Commercial varieties are chance seedlings selected for superior fruit or plant characteristics.

I grow 'Smoky', a purple-black fruit that has the highest sugar-to-acid ratio. It grows 2.5 m (8 ft) tall and 2 m (6.5 ft) wide. 'Regent' is a smaller shrub growing 1.5 m (5 ft) tall and wide.

In the Garden

Saskatoons are grown from root divisions and root and softwood cuttings. Plants grown from seed do not have the same characteristics as their parents. Plant saskatoons in full sun, fertilize with compost and manure every spring.

Saskatoons have beautiful white flowers in early spring, and for this reason I would grow them even if they didn't have berries with a sweet almond taste.

Pruning

Saskatoons produce their best fruit on shoots that are two to four years old.

In the Kitchen

Eat raw or add to pancakes, muffins, cakes and pies.

Harvesting and Preserving

Saskatoons ripen in July. They can be frozen or made into jam (see Freezer Garden Berry Jam, page 169).

Energy Snack

Pemmican, a mixture made of pounded dried meat, animal fat and dried fruit, usually saskatoons, is a high-energy food traditionally made by First Nations. Later, European explorers and fur traders began to eat it.

STRAWBERRY: *Fragaria × ananassa* (perennial)

Strawberries multiply by putting out long shoots or runners that grow other plants throughout the growing season. One of your neighbours or a friend will probably have runners to spare. Or head to your nursery and look for the cultivars 'Ogallala', 'Tristar' and 'Seascape'.

In the Garden

Plant seedlings as soon as the soil is dry enough to be workable. Choose a spot in full sun with ordinary fertile garden soil. Fertilize with compost or rotted manure at planting time and again every spring thereafter. But no more than that, as too much fertilizer grows big, tasteless berries, and there are plenty of those at the supermarket. Plant seedlings so their crowns, the spot where the stems grow from the root, are just above soil level.

Nurseries sell strawberries in hanging baskets and pots. Enjoy all summer and remember to plant them into the garden before winter so you can enjoy them again next year.

With a bit of extra work, you can increase your strawberry crop by picking off all flowers and runners the first year to help the plants gain strength.

The second year, harvest berries and cut off runners until late summer/early fall when runners can be planted in a new bed for a future crop. Many hybrids don't last more than a few years, so you will have to pay attention and toss on the compost any non-producing, worn-out plants.

In the Kitchen

Eat fresh while out gardening, or with cream, chocolate or ice cream.

Harvesting and Preserving

Strawberries ripen from mid-July onward until killed by frost. They are best frozen or made into jam (see Freezer Garden Berry Jam, page 169).

Pull fresh strawberries off the plant to eat while working in the garden.

Four-Season Eating for the Cold-Climate Gardener

SIMPLE WAYS TO ENJOY THE BOUNTY OF YOUR GARDEN THROUGHOUT THE YEAR

*T*he recipes in this section take you through a full northern gardening year and are arranged by season. As the food in your garden is ready for harvest, it will be easy to find corresponding recipes.

Who wants to be inside cooking when the sun is shining? Summer is too short to spend by the hot stove turning garden produce into gourmet dishes—better to take a couple minutes to blanch it and tuck it into the freezer for winter cooking. In summer, you will mostly be making basic condiments to use for salads and barbecues. Fall is the time to flavour oils and make pesto, along with fermented foods. During winter and through to next spring— a long and dark span of icy days—you will dig into your stash of frozen, dried and root-cellared or cold-roomed herbs and vegetables to create delicious garden-centred meals every day no matter what the weather.

Effortless Kitchen Gear

Knowing what utensils a cook uses provides insight into how they prepare food.

I use a well-seasoned cast iron pan for stir-frying, sautéing and making omelettes. Nothing sticks to it, the pan heats up evenly and retains heat, and I can put it in the oven or under the broiler. I may use a tablespoon of oil or butter for flavour. The best cast iron pots come with an oven-friendly lid—use the pot on top of the stove first to brown and caramelize ingredients, and then put it into the oven to bake food slowly.

I use a mortar and pestle made of heavy stone to smash small quantities of garlic, herbs, chilies and spices. For crushing large quantities, I use a blender; and I also use my blender for puréeing soup (I purée a cup at a time on low, gradually increasing the speed so it doesn't splatter), making pesto and pistou, mayonnaise and sauces.

A sharp knife is essential: get one made of carbon steel that can be sharpened, and use it to chop vegetables or finely dice herbs.

A Few Notes about these Recipes

Recipes are intended only as inspiration. Ingredient amounts in my recipes are suggestions only and can be adjusted according to your taste, or adapted to what is ready to eat in your garden or what food you've stored for the winter.

The recipes assume washing of all edible flowers, fruits and vegetables before using, and removing any hard or fibrous stem parts.

CHAPTER 10

Spring Starts: Late April into June

IN THE SPRING GARDEN, PERENNIAL VEGETABLES AND HERBS START GROWING BENEATH THE SNOW, FORCING STALKS SKYWARD IN SEARCH OF SUNSHINE

*D*espite icy winds and my frozen fingers, I spend lots of time outside in the spring garden eagerly pushing aside the snow and poking around the perennial crowns, looking for signs of growth. Those longed-for first spring greens are welcome to my green-starved senses.

In northern gardens, spring is spent mostly waiting for the snow to melt and the frost to come out of the ground—once this happens, everything goes into overdrive as the plants compete for space and sunshine. Spring turns into summer in just a few days.

Tightly furled rhubarb emerges early each spring.

FIRST SIGN OF SPRING SALAD

Dressing
½ tsp (2.5 mL) olive oil
1 tsp (5 mL) white wine or rice vinegar
½ tsp (2.5 mL) Dijon mustard, or more to
    taste

Salad
½ cup (125 mL) sorrel leaves
Handful of chives, chopped
Salt and pepper to taste

This is the first salad I make from my garden every year. Even before the snow melts away from their crowns, sorrel and chives are already growing. My initial spring harvest consists of only a handful of leaves and a tablespoon or two of chopped chives—but it's enough. This recipe feeds one and is easily multiplied for more diners.

1. To make the dressing, whisk together olive oil, vinegar and Dijon mustard.
2. In a small bowl, toss whole sorrel leaves and chopped chives.
3. Pour the dressing over the greens, tossing to ensure they are coated evenly and thinly.
4. Add salt and pepper to taste.

MAKES ONE SERVING

Sorrel is one of the first joys of spring.

RHUBARB CRUMBLE

When rhubarb stalks are a few inches high, you can start harvesting. I'm so impatient that I usually start cutting them when they are only three inches. Rhubarb leaves are poisonous, so eat the stalks only; add leaves to your compost. Once rhubarb becomes abundant, chop and freeze some of the stalks so that you can make this dish for a midwinter treat. Note that new rhubarb stalks take less time to cook than older, tougher stalks.

I prefer the sharpness of unadulterated rhubarb, relying on the sugar in the topping for sweetness, but feel free to adjust the sweetener to your own preference, adding up to 1 cup (250 mL) of sugar, or a combination of sugar and a sweet fruit like chopped apples. The amount of rhubarb depends on how much you have. If you are like me, you won't have much on your first harvest—you can always adjust topping ingredient quantities accordingly.

1. For the filling: In a medium bowl, combine rhubarb, spices, and sugar if desired. Pile into a 8 x 8 in (20 cm x 20 cm) baking dish.
2. For the topping: melt butter in a medium pot. Remove from heat and stir in oats and brown sugar, mixing together until the mixture forms a crumbly mass.
3. Spread the topping over the rhubarb filling.
4. Bake at 350F (175C) for 45 minutes or until the crumble is golden brown and rhubarb bubbles up at the sides of the dish. Cover with foil if the topping browns too quickly.
5. Alternatively, cook in a microwave on high for 6 to 7 minutes, until the rhubarb starts to bubble.

MAKES FOUR SERVINGS

Filling
4 cups (1 L) rhubarb, cut into ½-in (1-cm) slices
Ground cinnamon or cardamom to taste
Up to 1 cup (250 mL) sugar or other sweetener

Topping
⅓ cup (80 mL) butter
2½ cups (600 mL) rolled oats
1 cup (250 mL) packed brown sugar, or more to taste

I look forward to juicy and sour rhubarb baked with brown sugar and oats in my first spring crumble.

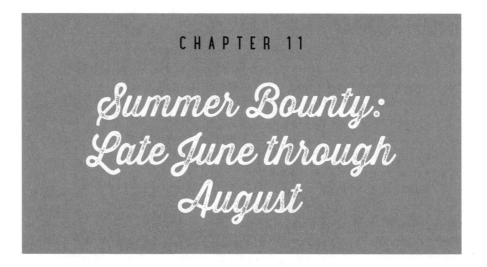

CHAPTER 11

Summer Bounty: Late June through August

SUMMER IS FINALLY HERE—THE DAYS ARE LONG AND WARM, GARDEN PRODUCE IS CONTINUALLY RIPENING AND THE HARVEST IS PICKED DAILY

*S*ummer offers an abundance of fresh flavour. It's a pleasure to harvest a few mint leaves for an early-morning cup of herbal tea, nasturtium flowers and leaves to add flavour and colour to a lunchtime fresh-from-the-garden salad and edible violets to jazz up my evening cocktail.

Edible flowers are easy to grow and add beauty and zest to sweet and savoury dishes.

FLOWER AND HERB VINEGAR

. . . .

Choose mild vinegar, like white wine or rice, to allow the taste of herbs or edible flowers to shine through.

1 cup (250 mL) flowers and herbs (see sidebar)
2 cups (475 mL) white wine or rice vinegar

1. Place flowers in a sterilized 2-cup (475-mL) canning jar. Heat vinegar to just below boiling point (195F/90C) and gently pour. Seal with lid.
2. Leave in a warm place for a week or two, shaking occasionally, until desired colour and taste is reached. Pour through a sieve to filter out the flowers; discard them into the compost. Place vinegar in a new sterilized jar.
3. Store in a cool, dark place to keep the colour bright. Vinegar will keep for up to 8 months.

MAKES 2 CUPS (475 ML)

Flower and Flavour Picks for Vinegar

Borage Flowers: Blue-tinged vinegar with a cucumber taste, for spring salads.

Whole Chili: Searing-hot vinegar—leave the chili in the jar so you remember what it is. Use to add spice to long-simmering stews and egg dishes.

Chive Flowers: A pinky-purple vinegar with an oniony taste; great as a dressing for coleslaw.

Dill Weed: Delicate yellow flowers and green leaves with the taste of pickles; use in salad dressings.

Lemon Balm/Lemon Thyme Leaves: Use together or singly for a lemon-scented experience; add tang to curries and stir-fried vegetables.

Lovage Leaves: Add a celery-like taste; great in soups.

Nasturtium Flowers: Turns a lovely jewel-like shade of orange-red; the more flowers you use, the deeper the colour. The spicy, peppery taste is perfect for salad dressings and bean dishes.

Tarragon Leaves: This infused vinegar is traditional and wonderful flavouring in stews and soups.

FLOWER SALAD

Edible Flowers or Petals

Borage

Calendula (petals only, discard the centre)

Chive (chopped)

Dianthus

Lavender

Nasturtium

Edible Pea

Rose (petals only, discard the centre)

Violet

Cut-and-Come-Again Greens (torn into bite-sized pieces)

Arugula

Beet tops

Collards

Kale

Lettuce

Sorrel

Spinach

Swiss chard

Garden Delicacies (chopped as needed)

Bulb or green onions

Peas and/or edible pea pods

Succulent shoots of cauliflower, broccoli and broccoli rabe

Herbs (finely chopped)

Basil

Borage (1–2 leaves only)

Chive

Cilantro

Dill

Lovage (1–2 leaves only)

Nasturtium leaves

Parsley

By now, you will be harvesting the first edible flowers and tender leaves of baby greens—cut back by a third with scissors to keep them young and succulent. When making salads, there are no rules: go wild and invent new ways of combining the many ingredients a garden provides throughout this season. Harvest in the early morning or late afternoon for the crispest leaves and flowers. Rinse in cold water; use a salad spinner to dry.

1. In a bowl, combine 3 cups (700 mL) flowers and greens and ¼ cup (60 mL) herbs for each person. Refrigerate until it's time to dress the salad.
2. For each serving, add about 2 tablespoons (30 mL) Simple Salad Dressing (page 147), or the dressing of your choice, and toss to coat.

EACH SERVING MAKES A GENEROUS SIDE SALAD

Top: 'Carouby de Mausanne' snow pea produces two-toned edible flowers.

Left: Cos lettuce can be tossed with any and all of the edible flowers available in your garden.

SIMPLE SALAD DRESSING

Adjust these measurements according to how much salad you are making.

1. Whisk vinegar, oil and salt and pepper together, adjusting to taste.
2. Toss into the salad just prior to eating.

MAKES ENOUGH FOR ONE SIDE SERVING OF SALAD

{ 1–2 Tbsp (15–30 mL) Flower and Herb Vinegar (see Flower and Flavour Picks, page 145)
1 Tbsp (15 mL) olive oil
Salt and pepper to taste

BASIC MAYONNAISE

This is the basis for many sauces, dips and salad dressings. Vary it by changing the flavourings, adding herbs and/or more garlic, or dispensing with the mustard. Use apple cider, red wine, white wine or rice vinegar or your own herbal vinegar or lemon juice…in other words, experiment.

1. In a blender, process garlic, mustard, vinegar, egg and a small amount of oil.
2. Pour in remaining oil slowly and process until mixture starts to thicken, then stop immediately. Add salt and pepper to taste. Will keep in the refrigerator for up to 4 days.

MAKES ABOUT 1 CUP (250 ML)

{ 1 clove garlic, smashed
1 tsp (5 mL) Dijon mustard
1 Tbsp (15 mL) flavoured vinegar (see Flower and Flavour Picks, page 145)
1 egg *
½ –¾ cup (125–180 mL) olive oil
Salt and pepper to taste

Properly handled, a raw or lightly cooked Canada Grade 'A' egg is safe for healthy individuals. However, due to the small risk of contamination, eating raw eggs may not be appropriate for everyone, including very young children, the elderly or pregnant women.

My Inspiration for Cooking

My mother is a wonderfully creative cook. Every day of the week during my childhood, she made delicious meals with fresh ingredients, except for those rare occasions when Dad made one of his legendary curries. I credit my mother for my interest in preparing meals from scratch and depending on homemade condiments—like stock, pesto and mayonnaise. These basics are the foundation of fabulous-tasting food; once you have them, you can make anything.

COLOURFUL KALE CAESAR SALAD

Dressing

1 clove garlic, smashed

1 tsp (5 mL) Dijon mustard

1 Tbsp (15 mL) lemon juice

1 egg *

2 tsp (10 mL) anchovy paste or 2 anchovy
fillets

½ –¾ cup (125–180 mL) olive oil

Croutons

4–8 garlic cloves, smashed

¼ cup (60 mL) olive oil or butter

¼ cup (60 mL) chopped herbs

4 slices of bread, cubed

Salt and pepper to taste

Salad

8 cups (2 L) chopped or torn kale leaves

Grated Parmesan, Asiago, Romano or
other hard cheese to taste

Salt and pepper to taste

So just what is so great about kale? Kale is rich in vitamins K and C and calcium, and like other brassicas contains chemicals that possess cancer-fighting and cholesterol-lowering properties. Every part of this plant is edible—incorporate it into your diet as a substitute for lettuce, spinach, chard, bok choy and other greens. Choose a mixture of kale varieties for a colourful dish. For the croutons, use whatever herbs your garden offers, including rosemary, thyme, sage, savory, parsley and/or any favourites you might have.

1. For the dressing: in a blender, process garlic, mustard, lemon juice, egg, anchovy and a small amount of the oil. Pour in remaining oil slowly and process until mixture starts to thicken, then stop immediately.

2. For the croutons, sauté garlic in oil or butter until golden brown, mix in herbs, bread cubes, salt and pepper; stir until the bread has soaked up the mixture and is golden brown and crisp. Drain on paper towels.

3. In a large salad bowl, toss kale with dressing (to taste—you may not wish to use all the dressing; save any remainder in the fridge for up to a week), most of the croutons, cheese as desired, salt and pepper. Garnish with remaining croutons and a little more cheese.

MAKES FOUR SERVINGS

Properly handled, a raw or lightly cooked Canada Grade 'A' egg is safe for healthy individuals. However, due to the small risk of contamination, eating raw eggs may not be appropriate for everyone, including very young children, pregnant women or the elderly.

Kale—an all-purpose healthy green.

RADISH BITTER-GREEN STIR-FRY

The best way to eat radishes is one second after you've pulled them out of the ground and wiped off the dirt. Chomp down on the spicy root but don't stop there—radish greens are just as edible. Use them to make this dish or substitute bitter lettuce that has gone to seed or been touched by frost. Serve as a side dish at dinner or eat with a couple of fried eggs and salsa for breakfast or lunch.

2 Tbsp (30 mL) olive oil
2 Tbsp (30 mL) butter
8 cups (2 L) chopped radish greens or bitter lettuce
1 Tbsp (15 mL) lemon juice
Salt and pepper to taste

1. Pour oil into pan and add butter, heating until melted and bubbling, turning down heat so it doesn't brown. Pile chopped greens into pan, cooking until soft but still bright green.
2. Stir in lemon juice and sprinkle with salt and pepper. Eat immediately.

MAKES ONE TO TWO SERVINGS AS A MAIN, FOUR AS A SIDE

FRESH-LEAF HERBAL TEA

I like to make my herbal teas with fresh leaves—I've tried using dried leaves but the flavour is not the same.

1–2 Tbsp (15–30 mL) chopped fresh mint, lemon balm and/or lemon thyme
1 cup (250 mL) boiling water
Sugar or honey if desired, to taste
Edible flowers as garnish (optional)

1. Steep herbs in boiling water for 2 to 5 minutes until it has reached your preferred strength.
2. If desired, sweeten with sugar or honey to taste.
3. Serve hot, or cool and serve over ice. Garnish with edible flowers.

MAKES ONE SERVING

HERBED SALT

1 cup (250 mL) coarse kosher or sea salt
1 cup (250 mL) finely chopped dried herbs

I was given a jar of Fleur de Sel mixed with herbs as a Christmas present; once it was gone, I decided to emulate it. In France, this salt is harvested by hand from the Atlantic Ocean; instead, I used coarse kosher salt from the local grocery store. I added garden herbs that retain their flavour when dried, including rosemary, thyme, lavender, savory, sage and oregano. I prefer extra rosemary and just a little lavender in the herb mixture: try adding these ingredients in varying amounts until you come up with something that suits your own taste buds.

1. Mix salt and herbs together.
2. Pour into a jar with a tightly sealed lid and store in a cupboard. Keeps indefinitely.

MAKES ABOUT 2 CUPS (475 ML)

Using Herbed Salt

Spread about 2 tsp (10 mL) of Herbed Salt into your cast iron pan, using it instead of oil to sear and cook meat and fish. Sprinkle over bread dough or pizza before baking, or stir into casseroles, soups and stews.

STUFFED ZUCCHINI FLOWERS

As a lunch, appetizer or side, this dish is a bit fiddly but worth every minute of preparation time. Harvest as many flowers as you like—the plants will compensate by producing more.

1. Pull the insides out of the flowers to make room for the filling.
2. Mash filling ingredients together with a fork.
3. Spoon about 2 tablespoons (30 mL) filling into each flower, rolling the flower into a sausage shape around the filling.
4. Mix ingredients for tempura batter just before frying—note that the mixture will still be lumpy, but avoid over-mixing, as it makes the tempura heavy and stodgy.
5. Heat 2 to 3 in (5–7.5 cm) oil in a cast iron pot until a drop of water sizzles. Dip 2 to 3 flowers at a time into the batter and deep-fry quickly until golden brown. Drain on paper towels. To ensure the tempura is crispy and light, keep the batter cold by refrigerating it between flower dippings.

MAKES TWO TO THREE SERVINGS AS A SIDE; MORE AS AN APPETIZER

12–15 zucchini flowers

Cheese Filling
1 cup (250 mL) goat cheese
2 Tbsp (30 mL) minced chives
1–2 cloves garlic, smashed
1–2 Tbsp (15–30 mL) chopped basil
Salt and pepper to taste

Batter
1 cup (250 mL) rice or wheat flour, or tempura mix
1 cup (250 mL) soda water or other fizzy water, cold from the fridge
Canola oil for deep-frying

Lovely zucchini flowers.

GARLIC SCAPE STIR-FRY

1 Tbsp (15 mL) oil

1–2 tsp (5–10 mL) grated ginger

1 clove garlic, smashed

1 small onion, chopped

1 dozen garlic scapes, chopped into bite-sized pieces

Crushed red pepper to taste

Dash of soy sauce

½ tsp (2.5 mL) sugar

Splash of lime juice

Splash of fish sauce

Basil and cilantro, chopped, for garnish

One of the benefits of growing hardneck garlic is the scape—or flower shoot—it produces. The stalk twists into a spiral, so it's easy to know when it's scape-picking time—see photo on page xx). Jazz up this recipe by adding other vegetables like baby carrots, peas, beans, broccoli, cauliflower and chopped greens.

1. Heat oil until a drop of water sizzles. Sauté ginger, garlic and onion until soft and browning at the edges. Add garlic scapes and cook until fork-tender and bright green.
2. Toss with crushed red pepper, soy sauce, sugar, lime juice and fish sauce.
3. Garnish with basil and cilantro.

MAKES THREE TO FOUR SERVINGS

Harvest garlic scapes once the flower stalk has twisted around itself. Leave some scapes on the plant for bulbils, to plant for more garlic. Bulbils take two years to produce heads of garlic with multiple cloves.

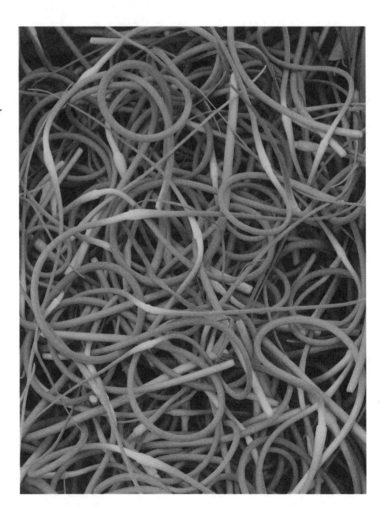

GRILLED VEGETABLE SALAD

Cooking vegetables caramelizes their inherent sugars, drawing out flavours which are accented by a homemade herb-filled dressing.

1. Combine dressing ingredients together in a lidded jar, cover and shake until mixed.
2. Cut larger vegetables—onions, zucchini and big potatoes and carrots—in half, keeping snow peas, beans and smaller asparagus whole. Brush with olive oil.
3. On a preheated barbecue, grill the vegetables until al dente (still slightly crisp) and brown around the edges. Remove from the barbecue and chop into bite-sized pieces.
4. Toss with dressing.
5. Arrange leafy greens on a platter, piling the barbecued vegetables on top.
6. Garnish with flowers and herbs.

MAKES FOUR SERVINGS

Dressing
2–3 Tbsp (30–45 mL) olive oil
3–4 Tbsp (45–60 mL) apple cider vinegar
1–2 tsp (5–10 mL) each of chopped rosemary, thyme, savory, sage and parsley
1–2 smashed garlic cloves
Salt and pepper to taste

Salad
4 cups (1 L) mixed vegetables: zucchini, asparagus, baby carrots, sugar snap peas, snow peas, beans, young onions, new potatoes, beets, fennel, broccoli or cauliflower.
Olive oil
4–5 large green leaves: kale, lettuce, spinach, Swiss chard or whatever you have in your garden
Edible flowers and sprigs of herbs for garnish

Eat grilled vegetables as a side dish or sprinkle with cheese for lunch.

BARBECUED LETTUCE

Mayonnaise
1 clove garlic, smashed
1 tsp (5 mL) Dijon mustard
1 Tbsp (15 mL) flavoured vinegar (see
   Flower and Flavour Picks, page 145)
1 egg *
1 tsp (5 mL) sugar
Dash of cayenne pepper
½ –¾ cup (125–180 mL) Herb Oil
   (page 157)
Salt and pepper to taste

1 mature romaine or cos lettuce

An Internet friend gave me this idea; while it may sound strange, it is fabulous.

1. Make the mayonnaise first. In a blender, process garlic, mustard, vinegar, egg, sugar, cayenne pepper and a small amount of oil. Pour in remaining oil slowly and process until mixture starts to thicken, then stop immediately. Add salt and pepper to taste.
2. Cut lettuce in half lengthwise and barbecue until it begins to brown. Flip over and cook until all sides are slightly brown.
3. Place each half on its own plate. Drizzle teaspoons of mayonnaise over the lettuce so it gets into all the layers.

MAKES TWO SERVINGS AS AN APPETIZER OR SIDE

Properly handled, a raw or lightly cooked Canada Grade 'A' egg is safe for healthy individuals. However, due to the small risk of contamination, eating raw eggs may not be appropriate for everyone, including very young children, pregnant women or the elderly.

Yes, you can barbecue lettuce.

NORTHERN GADO GADO

This salad is wonderful for lunch on a hot day. I've adapted the traditional Malaysian recipe to use the vegetables I grow in my northern garden—carrots, cabbage, broccoli, cauliflower, peppers, beans and peas all work very well. For greens, choose baby kale, sorrel, cabbage, spinach and/or lettuce. Peanut sauce is the customary accompaniment; make it first (see recipe below).

1. Chop mixed vegetables into same-sized pieces.
2. Fry tofu in oil for a few minutes until golden brown, drain on paper towel.
3. Steam vegetables briefly until they change colour but are still crunchy.
4. Arrange shredded greens on individual plates. Pile cooked vegetables and fried tofu on top. Pour warmed peanut sauce over top, to taste.
5. Garnish with cucumber, tomato, egg, basil and cilantro.

MAKES TWO SERVINGS

4 cups (1 L) of mixed vegetables
¼ cup (60 mL) tofu cut in ½-in (1-cm) slices
Olive oil for frying
2 cups (475 mL) shredded garden greens
Base kacang (Peanut Sauce) to taste (see below)
A few slices of cucumber
1 small tomato, sliced
1 boiled egg, sliced
Handful of basil, chopped
Handful of cilantro, chopped

BASE KACANG (PEANUT SAUCE)

The traditional accompaniment to gado gado. Look for the shrimp paste in the ethnic-foods aisle of your supermarket.

1. Stir-fry peanuts in oil for 4 minutes, until browned. Remove from oil and drain on paper towel. Pound, or grind in a blender, to make a coarse powder. Set aside.
2. Blend onion, garlic and shrimp paste in a blender with a little salt. Fry this mixture for 1 minute.
3. Add chilies, sugar, soy sauce and water to the mixture in the frying pan. Bring to a boil, and add the ground peanuts. Simmer until sauce becomes thick. Add lime juice and more salt to taste.
4. This peanut sauce will keep in the fridge for up to a week.

MAKES ABOUT 1½ CUPS (350 ML)

1½ cups (350 mL) raw peanuts
1 Tbsp (15 ml) oil
½ cup (125 mL) chopped onion
2 cloves garlic, smashed
1 tsp (5 mL) shrimp paste
Salt to taste
Chilies to taste, pounded in a mortar and pestle
1 tsp (5 mL) sugar
1 Tbsp (15 mL) soy sauce
1¼ cups (300 mL) water
1 Tbsp (15 mL) lime juice

CHAPTER 12

Fall Comforts: September through October

NOW IS THE TIME TO MAKE FLAVOURED OILS, PESTO, FERMENTED FOODS AND SOUPS FOR THE MONTHS AHEAD

Mornings are getting very chilly—often below zero Celsius—and the intermittent light frosts increase in frequency and intensity. Covering your tender plants at night ekes out more growing time, increasing your chance of harvesting a ripe crop.

Kale and other brassicas taste even better after being touched by frost.

HERB OIL

Any vegetable oil is suitable for steeping herbs, although I like to use extra virgin olive oil, especially if the mixture is destined for the salad bowl. Use singly or combine for an interesting taste sensation; add a little horseradish or garlic, if you like. Keep herbed oils in the fridge to prevent spoiling. I use my herbed oils to make salad dressings and mayonnaise, or drizzle it over fresh veggies for extra flavour.

> 2 cups (475 mL) chopped fresh herb leaves or 1 cup (250 mL) dried herbs (Try all your favourite herbs, including dill, basil, coriander, parsley, sage and sorrel.)
> ½ cup (125 mL) or more vegetable oil

1. In a 1-cup (250-mL) jar, mix herbs with enough oil to cover.
2. Keep in the fridge for up to a week if using fresh herbs, or for several months if using dried herbs. Freeze for longer storage.

Makes about ½ cup (125 mL) oil.

GARLIC OIL

Add small amounts of this oil to soups, stews, dips or any dish for extra flavour. Depending on the pungency of the oil and the dish you are making, you may not need to add any more garlic to your recipe.

> 6 garlic cloves, minced
> 1 cup (250 mL) vegetable oil

1. Pour oil over minced garlic and steep overnight in refrigerator. Leave garlic in the oil—no need to strain it out.
2. Keep for up to three days in the refrigerator or freeze for longer storage.

Makes 1 cup (250 mL) oil.

CHILI OIL

Use this just like you do the Garlic Oil, but where you want some heat. The number of chili peppers to use depends on how hot you like your food. Also, different chilies have different intensities of heat—jalapenos are relatively mild, cayenne hot, habanero the hottest.

> Dried chilies to taste
> 1 cup (250 mL) vegetable oil

1. Cut chilies in half and combine with oil in a 1-cup (250-mL) canning jar. Be careful not to touch your face or eyes during this process; you may also want to wear gloves to protect your hands.
2. Steep the oil overnight in the refrigerator. Leave chilies in the oil—no need to strain out.
3. Keep in the fridge for up to one month, or freeze for longer storage.

Makes 1 cup (250 mL) oil.

GARDEN PESTO (OR PISTOU)

3 Tbsp (45 mL) pine nuts (or other nut)

2 cups (475 mL) basil leaves (or other herb)

5 cloves garlic, smashed

½ cup (125 mL) olive oil

1 cup (250 mL) grated Parmesan, Asiago, Romano or other hard cheese (optional)

Preserve herbs by mixing them with oil and garlic to make a paste called "pesto" or "pistou": "pesto" is traditionally made in Italy; "pistou" in Provence. In September, before frost kills my basil, I process all that remains of my crop with garlic, olive oil and pine nuts (and/or hazelnuts, almonds or sunflower seeds, depending on what I have), packing it into freezer bags or canning jars for freezing. In the middle of winter I hack off a piece to use for pasta sauce or to flavour other dishes (see sidebar). Basil is traditional, but you can make pesto/pistou with any herb—try mint, arugula or parsley. If you are freezing pesto/pistou, leave out the cheese—add it later when you make your pasta.

1. Toast the nuts over medium heat, stirring frequently, until just golden and fragrant, about 5 minutes.
2. Add all ingredients to a food processor or blender. Purée.
3. Use immediately, store for a few days in the fridge with a layer of oil on top, or freeze (leaving room in the jar or bag for expansion).

MAKES 2 CUPS (475 ML)

Frozen pesto or pistou brings the flavour of summer to my winter cooking.

Ways to Eat Pesto and Pistou

Other than as a traditional sauce for pasta, there are many ways to eat pesto and pistou. A tablespoon or so can be used to:

- *Flavour soups or stews just before serving*
- *Marinate and glaze roasted meats*
- *Drizzle over pizza or tomato dishes*
- *Flavour salad dressings*
- *Act as a base for a dip to serve with crudités or chips*

SEASON'S END SOUP WITH PISTOU

This is great for using up whatever vegetables you have hanging around your garden this time of year, including over-ripe peas and beans, carrots, potatoes, onions, frosted lettuce, cabbage, broccoli and kale, ripe and green tomatoes and zucchini that's grown to football size. Or you can make this delicious soup anytime with any vegetables. Separate root vegetables and tomatoes from leafy vegetables, as they are added at different stages of cooking.

1. Sauté garlic and onion in oil until soft.
2. Stir in root vegetables and/or tomatoes, rice and/or barley (if using) and beans (if using). Add stock and bring to a boil, then turn down heat to let soup simmer until rice and barley are cooked and vegetables tender.
3. Add the more tender vegetables such as peas, green beans, zucchini and/or leafy greens and pasta (if using); simmer for about 10 minutes or until pasta is al dente.
4. Remove pot from heat. Stir in pistou and salt and pepper to taste.
5. Ladle into bowls and top with cheese.

MAKES TWO SERVINGS

1–2 garlic cloves, smashed
1 onion, chopped
1 Tbsp (15 mL) oil
2 cups (475 mL) diced vegetables, separated
¼ cup (60 mL) rice, barley or both (optional)
½ cup (125 mL) kidney, garbanzo, pinto, black or white beans, cooked and drained (optional)
2–4 cups (475 mL–1 L) stock
½ cup (125 mL) dried pasta (optional)
¼ cup (60 mL) Garden Pesto (page 158), made without cheese
Salt and pepper to taste
Grated Parmesan, Asiago, Romano or other hard cheese to taste

When temperatures hover around zero, hot soup is the perfect antidote to a cold day spent cleaning up the garden.

ROSEHIP HERBAL TEA

1 cup (250 mL) boiling water
1½ Tbsp (23 mL) ground rosehips
1 Tbsp (15 mL) dried herbs (optional)

Drying Herbs for Tea: Dry leaves in a shaded spot outdoors or indoors until dry and crumbly. Store in an airtight container in a dark cupboard.

Anxious to ensure her girls got all their nutrients, my mother made juice from rosehip syrup she purchased. Very high in vitamin C, rosehips proliferate in my garden and I gather them every fall for a healthful tea. When harvesting, trim off the stem and blossom end, cut the hips in half and scoop out the seeds. Lay the halved hips in a shaded, airy place outdoors or indoors until they are hard and dry. Store in a jar in a dark cupboard. For a fresher taste, grind the hips in a coffee grinder just prior to brewing the tea. Adding dried herbs makes it even tastier—try mint, lemon thyme and lemon balm.

1. Add boiling water to the ground rosehips and steep for 10 minutes. Stir in dried herbs for additional flavour.

MAKES ONE SERVING

Rosehips in the fall garden.

CARAMELIZED ROASTED VEGETABLES

Perfectly roasted vegetables are crisp on the outside and tender on the inside. Their natural sugars melt in the oven heat, adding depth and complexity. Make this in the first cold days of autumn, all winter, and in chilly early spring when you harvest overwintered root veggies from your garden. Use whatever you have on hand: Jerusalem artichokes, carrots, parsnips, rutabagas, garlic, turnips, beets, onions, potatoes and/or tomatoes. Sprinkle cooked vegetables, hot from the oven, with salt and pepper. Serve with Colourful Kale Caesar Salad (page 148) and grilled meats or Green Eggs and Bacon (page 171).

1. Chop vegetables (except tomatoes) into pieces about 1×2 in (2.5x5 cm).
2. Brush whole garlic cloves and all sides of vegetables with oil and place in a single layer in a roasting dish.
3. Roast at 350F (175C) for 30 minutes to an hour, until a fork spears the vegetables easily and they are getting crispy around the edges—the fresher the vegetables the quicker they will cook.
4. Add salt and pepper to taste.

MAKES TWO SERVINGS AS A SIDE DISH

4 cups (1 L) vegetables
Garlic cloves, peeled, whole
Olive oil for brushing
Salt and pepper to taste

Roast tomatoes whole and chop them up a little when you bring them out of the oven—this will release their juices, flavouring the dish.

SPICY CABBAGE SAUTÉ

This was inspired by a recipe found on Molly Wizenberg's blog, Orangette. Her anecdotal writing style endeared itself to me and I'm an avid reader—most of her entries are about food. Serve this dish as a side or alongside an egg for a nourishing lunch.

1. Heat oil and sauté cabbage, onion, garlic and carrot (if using) until tender and edges of the vegetables are starting to brown.
2. Stir in Sambal Oelek to taste and add a dash or so of soy sauce.

MAKES TWO SERVINGS

1 Tbsp (15 mL) oil
1 small or ½ large cabbage, shredded
½ cup (125 mL) chopped onion
1 garlic clove, smashed
1–2 carrots, cut into thin matchsticks 2 in (5 cm) long (optional)
1–2 tsp (5–10 mL) Sambal Oelek (see sidebar), or to taste
1–2 dashes soy sauce

Sambal Oelek

In Malaysia, where I lived for four years, a small dish of Sambal Oelek—a paste made of mashed chilies, lime juice and salt—was present on every table of every restaurant, much like salt and pepper in North America. You can buy Sambal Oelek at most supermarkets.

FERMENTED HOT PEPPERS

12 hot peppers, sliced into rings
½ in (1 cm) ginger, sliced
½ tsp (2.5 mL) black mustard seed
Salt

Sandor Ellix Katz's *The Art of Fermentation* is the quintessential reference on fermented food, and I've adapted this recipe from his book. It's great as a sambal (page 161), to add fire to curries when the other diners don't like spice.

1. Layer peppers and ginger in a 1-cup (250-mL) canning jar, sprinkling mustard seed and ½ tsp (2.5 mL) salt on each pepper layer.
2. Screw on the lid.
3. Place on a kitchen counter. Shake every day and unscrew lid to let gas escape. Taste and stir peppers daily, adding more salt if liquid is insufficient to coat peppers.
4. After a week or when the peppers have reached your desired flavour, move into the fridge. They last several months.

MAKES 1 CUP (250 ML)

SPICY CABBAGE FERMENT

1 cabbage, shredded
2 carrots, grated
4 garlic cloves, smashed
1 onion, sliced
1 in (2.5 cm) ginger, chopped finely
Hot peppers to taste, sliced
Salt

My take on a spicy Korean kimchee. Eat as a side dish to add spice and crunch to a meal.

1. Stir all ingredients except salt together and layer into a crock or basin, sprinkling ½ Tbsp (7.5 mL) salt over each ½-in (1-cm) layer.
2. Stir and taste every day, adding more salt if there isn't enough liquid to coat the vegetables.
3. After two or more weeks, when the mixture tastes sour, decant into a canning jar and refrigerate. Will keep for several months.

MAKES ONE CROCKFUL

"REAL" SAUERKRAUT

The real thing. Unlike commercial sauerkraut, this recipe does not rely on vinegar to preserve the cabbage. Because vinegar is used in commercial preparations, I shunned sauerkraut until I discovered this method of making it.

1 red or green cabbage
Salt

1. Shred cabbage, layer ½-in (1-cm) thick in crock or other deep ceramic basin. Sprinkle ½ tsp (2.5 mL) salt between each layer.
2. Press a plate, just small enough to fit inside the crock, on top of the cabbage, weighing it down with something heavy. Cover with a tea towel and place on the kitchen counter.
3. Stir every day. The salt should extract liquid from the cabbage—enough to coat it; if not, add more salt.
4. Taste every day, until desired sourness has been reached, usually within a couple of weeks.

MAKES ONE CROCKFUL

The best sauerkraut is made without vinegar.

GREEN TOMATO SOUP WITH PESTO

Olive oil for sautéing

1 cup (250 mL) onion, chopped

1 garlic clove, smashed

2 cups (475 mL) green tomatoes, roughly chopped

2 cups (475 mL) stock (any kind)

2 Tbsp (30 mL) Garden Pesto (page 158)

Salt and pepper to taste

Grated Parmesan, Asiago, Romano or other hard cheese for garnish

Here's how to use up all those green tomatoes that never made it to full size. If you're using cherry or grape tomatoes, don't bother chopping them. Tastes great with crisp pappadums (Indian lentil crackers) or crusty rolls.

1. Heat oil and sauté chopped onion until soft. Stir in garlic and green tomatoes; sauté a couple more minutes.
2. Add stock, bring to a boil, then reduce heat to allow it to simmer for 30 minutes until tomatoes are soft and falling apart.
3. Stir in pesto, salt and pepper to taste.
4. Ladle into bowls and garnish with cheese.

MAKES TWO SERVINGS

FRIED GREEN TOMATOES

4–5 green tomatoes, sliced ¼ in (½ cm) thick

Water for moistening

¾ cup (180 mL) cornmeal

Olive oil for frying

Salt

Spicy dipping sauce (see sidebar)

This is so good that you will deliberately not let any of your tomatoes ripen.

1. Dip tomato slices in water to moisten them. Dredge each slice in cornmeal, covering completely.
2. Pour a scant layer of oil into a frying pan and heat until a drop of water sizzles. Fry dredged tomato slices until golden and crispy. Sprinkle with salt.
3. Serve hot with spicy dipping sauce.

MAKES TWO SERVINGS AS AN APPETIZER OR SIDE DISH

> **Spicy Dipping Sauce**
>
> *To make a spicy dipping sauce, make Basic Mayonnaise (page 147), spicing it up with 1–2 tsp (5–10 mL) or more Chili Oil (page 157), Sambal Oelek, or other hot sauce.*

If frying up a big batch of tomatoes for a crowd, transfer tomatoes to a cookie rack on a baking tray and keep warm in the oven.

TORTILLA ESPAÑOLA

The traditional way to make an authentic Spanish omelette—serve for lunch or eat as tapas. A good way to use lots of fresh garden herbs.

Oil for frying

3–4 potatoes, cut in half and sliced ¼-in (½-cm) thick

1 onion, cut in half and sliced ¼-in (½-cm) thick

4 eggs

Salt and pepper to taste

Herbs for garnish: parsley, basil, rosemary and sage

1. Pour a scant layer of oil in frying pan and heat until a drop of water sizzles. Sauté potatoes and onions until soft. Transfer to a plate.
2. Beat eggs until frothy; season with salt and pepper.
3. Mix potatoes and onions with eggs.
4. Heat 1 Tbsp (15 mL) of oil in pan; when hot, pour in egg mixture. Cover the pan and cook on moderate heat until done.
5. Flip out of pan onto plate. Garnish with chopped herbs. Eat hot or cold, cut into wedges.

MAKES TWO SERVINGS FOR LUNCH, FOUR OR MORE AS TAPAS

GRATED BEETS WITH GARLIC AND YOGURT

Serve on Valentine's Day or any dark winter day when you need a tasty hit of colour to liven up the dinner table. Serve with crudités, corn chips or crackers, or as a side dish with grilled or roasted meats.

2 small beets or 1 large, grated

1 clove of garlic, minced

2–3 Tbsp (30–45 mL) yogurt

1. Mix everything together in a bowl and serve.

MAKES ABOUT 1 CUP (250 ML).

Beets brighten up a dark winter day.

LATE-HARVEST RATATOUILLE

Olive oil for sautéing

1 onion, halved and sliced into half rings

4 cloves garlic, smashed

5 small zucchini, cut in half then into ½-in (1-cm) slices

1 to 2 Tbsp (15–30 mL) water

5 ripe tomatoes, chopped

1 Tbsp (15 mL) fresh herbs like sage, oregano and rosemary, chopped

Salt and pepper to taste

4–5 green, red or yellow peppers, deseeded and chopped into 2-in (5-cm) pieces

Grated Parmesan, Asiago, Romano or other hard cheese for garnish (optional)

The perfect blend of acidy tomatoes, sautéed garlic, caramelized onions, fresh peppers and browned zucchini and herbs. Eat it on its own, use as a topping for pizza, or enjoy with barbecued or grilled meats—tastes great with lamb.

1. Pour scant layer of oil in frying pan and heat until a drop of water sizzles. Sauté onions and garlic in oil until soft.
2. Add zucchini; stir until soft and starting to brown. Deglaze pan with water. Throw in tomatoes, herbs, salt and pepper to taste. Continue to sauté until tomatoes have broken down.
3. Add peppers, stirring until they are starting to get soft but still have their bright colours.
4. Adjust seasonings if desired. Serve plain or sprinkled with cheese.

MAKES UP TO FIVE SERVINGS AS A SIDE, TWO AS A MAIN

Peppers, onions, tomatoes and zucchini all seem to ripen at once, making ratatouille logical and delicious.

BAKED TOMATOES WITH FETA CHEESE

Make this in September when tomatoes are plentiful; or harvest from your stash of frozen tomatoes. This is quintessential cooking for cold weather—deep, earthy and warm.

4–5 large tomatoes, fresh or frozen
¼ cup (60 mL) olive oil
Salt and pepper
2–3 garlic cloves, smashed
1 cup (250 mL) feta cheese, chopped
2–3 Tbsp (30–45 mL) chopped parsley
Healthy splash of lemon juice

1. Place tomatoes on the bottom of a covered baking dish. Add olive oil, salt and pepper. Cover.
2. Bake at 450F (230C) for 20 minutes or longer, until tomatoes are soft and juicy.
3. Remove from oven, chop up the tomatoes a little, and stir in chopped feta, smashed garlic, parsley and lemon juice. Cover, return to oven and bake 15 minutes or until the cheese is melting and everything has melded into deliciousness.
4. Serve in bowls with slices of crusty bread or rolls to mop up the tomato juices. Or, as one friend suggests, over rice.

MAKES TWO SERVINGS

Variations on this Delicious Theme

- *Before putting the tomatoes back into the oven for the second time, add 1 cup (250 mL) shrimp, prawns or chopped fish. Remove from oven when fish is cooked.*

- *Increase the spicy heat by stirring in 1–2 tsp (5–10 mL) of Chili Oil (page 157) or Fermented Hot Peppers (page 162) before returning to the oven for the second time.*

- *Add 2 cups (475 mL) chopped green beans along with the feta and garlic.*

CHAPTER 13

Winter Warmers: November through April

WHEN THE GARDEN IS FROZEN IN WINTER, EAT FROM THE FREEZER AND FORAGE FROM YOUR COLD ROOM

*W*inter drags on and on. By the end of December, the sun barely crests the horizon. By March, warmer sunshine starts cracking the ice but it's a slow thaw fraught with alternating freezing rain and obliterating blizzards. Eat from your freezer and cold room to savour the tastes of your garden even through darkest winter. With foresight you will have stashed away ingredients for lots of scrumptious meals.

An assortment of freezer jam is a sweet reminder of summer.

FREEZER GARDEN BERRY JAM

Harvest from your stockpile of frozen saskatoons, cherries, blueberries, raspberries and strawberries for this fresh-tasting jam.

> 4 cups (1 L) berry fruit
> Zest and juice of 1 lemon
> Sugar—see steps for amount

1. Place the fruit in a medium pot and add the lemon zest and juice—this helps the jam to thicken. Gently simmer until the juice has emerged and fruit is wilted and soft, about 15 minutes. Once the berries have cooked down to this stage, measure the amount of fruit and juice you have, and add three-quarters that amount of sugar; for example, 4 cups (1 L) of cooked fruit requires 3 cups (700 mL) of sugar.
2. Boil rapidly until the jam coats the back of a spoon. Pour into canning jars, leaving ½ in (1 cm) headroom for expansion in the freezer. Screw on lids, cool and then tuck into your freezer.

MAKES ABOUT 6 CUPS (1.4 L)

BRASSICA BAKE

This idea is from a Flickr friend. Eat it as a lunch or serve as a side.

> 1 large or 2–3 smaller cauliflower or broccoli crowns , cut into florets
> 3–4 whole garlic cloves, peeled
> 1 cup (250 mL) Greek or full-fat yogurt or sour cream
> 1–2 cups (250–475 mL) grated sharp cheddar cheese, divided
> Cayenne pepper or paprika to taste

1. Steam cauliflower or broccoli and garlic cloves until soft.
2. Purée with potato masher. Mix with sour cream or yogurt and two thirds of the cheese.
3. Pile into a baking dish. Sprinkle with remaining cheese and garnish with cayenne pepper or paprika.
4. Bake in a 350F (175C) oven for 45 minutes to an hour, until bubbling and slightly browned on top.

MAKES TWO TO FOUR SERVINGS

Baked Garlic—So Easy and Good

Whenever the oven is on, consider baking garlic—it's an easy appetizer for a party, romantic dinner or family gathering. Simply slice off the top, wrap in foil and bake the whole head of garlic in a 350F (175C) oven until soft—about 1 hour. Spread on crackers, smear over roasted vegetables, or serve as a accompaniment to roasted or grilled meats.

WINTER SALAD

Dressing
1 Tbsp (15 mL) Herb Oil (page 157)
1 Tbsp (15 mL) Flower and Herb Vinegar, page 145)
1 clove garlic, smashed

Salad
1 fennel bulb, cut into matchsticks
1 onion, finely chopped
1 small or ½ large cabbage, shredded
1 carrot, cut into matchsticks.
Salt and pepper to taste
Chopped parsley for garnish

This satisfies my craving for something crunchy on days when the sun is buried beneath a blanket of grey, there's a metre of fresh snow on the ground and it's a bitterly cold -20C. Hopefully, your parsley can be snipped from a plant you had the foresight to dig up and pot inside last fall before the ground froze.

1. For the dressing, mix together oil, vinegar and garlic in a small jar with a lid. Shake well.
2. For the salad, pile chopped vegetables into a generous bowl. Sprinkle with salt and pepper.
3. Pour the dressing over vegetables, tossing together. Garnish with parsley and serve immediately.

MAKES FOUR TO SIX SERVINGS AS A SIDE

PURÉED BEET SOUP

1 Tbsp (15 mL) oil
½ onion, chopped
1 clove garlic, smashed
2 cups (475 mL) shredded cabbage
2 cups (475 mL) chopped beets
1 carrot, chopped
2 cups (475 mL) stock
Salt and pepper to taste
1–2 tsp (5–10 mL) finely minced dill weed or seed
1–2 Tbsp (15–30 mL) yogurt (optional)
Dash of cayenne pepper

Browned onions, garlic and cabbage sweeten the flavour of this soup, while cayenne pepper warms it up—it's the perfect antidote for a dark, frigid day.

1. Heat oil and sauté onion, garlic and cabbage in a medium pot until soft and slightly brown around the edges.
2. Add beet and carrot, sautéing briefly.
3. Pour in stock, add salt and pepper to taste, and bring to a boil. Reduce heat and simmer until vegetables are soft.
4. Allow to cool and purée in blender until smooth. Return to pot and reheat.
5. Stir in chopped dill weed or seed, taste and adjust salt and pepper if needed. Serve in bowls with a dollop of yogurt (if desired) and sprinkling of cayenne pepper.

MAKES TWO SERVINGS AS A MAIN, FOUR AS A STARTER OR SIDE

Alternate Toppings
- *In a small pan over medium-low heat, toast 1 tsp (5 mL) each of cumin seed and mustard seed in 1 Tbsp (15 mL) hot oil for just a few minutes, shaking the pan a little. Drizzle over the soup.*
- *Substitute the dollop of yogurt with a healthy dash of lemon juice.*

GREEN EGGS AND BACON

My take on the classic Dr. Seuss story. To green up your eggs, choose from kale, collard greens, spinach, chard, broccoli rabe and/or cabbage. For cheese, use what you have—blue cheese is especially toothsome.

4 or more slices bacon
1 small onion or ½ large onion, sliced
4 cups (1 L) roughly chopped greens
4 eggs, beaten
Salt and pepper
¹/₃ cup (80 mL) grated or sliced cheese

1. Fry bacon until crisp (retaining the fat); break into pieces.
2. Sauté onion in a little of the bacon fat (retaining 1 tsp/5 mL) until it starts to brown around the edges. Add greens and remaining 1 tsp (5 mL) bacon fat and sauté until wilted.
3. Beat together eggs until foamy, adding a dash of salt and pepper.
4. Spread sautéed vegetables over the bottom of the pan, arrange bacon pieces over top, and gently pour the eggs over the arrangement. Top with cheese and cook gently on medium-low heat until egg is set.

MAKES TWO SERVINGS AS A MAIN, FOUR AS A SIDE

Use fresh or frozen greens.

REMEMBERING SUMMER TOMATO SOUP

4–5 frozen tomatoes
¼ cup (60 mL) water
1 Tbsp (15 mL) oil
1 onion, chopped
2 cloves garlic, smashed
4 cups (1 L) soup stock
Salt and pepper to taste
2 Tbsp (30 mL) Garden Pesto (page 158),
    made without cheese (or substitute
    2 tsp/10 mL finely minced dill weed)
Grated Parmesan, Asiago, Romano or
    other hard cheese for garnish

It's December—the snow-covered ground is frozen solid and the thermometer's mercury is hardly visible. Take advantage of the tomatoes, pistou and soup stock stashed in your freezer, and garlic and onions dormant in your cold room to evoke a long-ago memory of summer.

1. Simmer tomatoes in water in a medium lidded pot until thawed. Transfer tomatoes and liquid into blender to cool before you process.
2. In your pot, heat oil and sauté onion and garlic until just golden. Add to tomatoes in blender and process until smooth.
3. Return tomato mixture to pot, pour in stock and salt and pepper to taste. Simmer gently 5–10 minutes or until heated through. Stir in pesto or dill weed. Serve topped with cheese.

MAKES TWO SERVINGS

BUBBLE AND SQUEAK

2–4 potatoes
½ large or 1 medium onion, sliced
2–4 cups (475 mL–1 L) shredded cabbage
1 Tbsp (15 mL) oil

I remember my mother making this—the name refers to the sound the cabbage makes as it is being cooked with the potatoes. A great way to use up leftover boiled potatoes. Eat with bangers (sausages).

1. Boil potatoes until soft.
2. In a large frying pan, sauté onion and cabbage in oil until soft.
3. Add potatoes, mashing them into the cabbage and onion. Cook like a giant pancake, flipping when the bottom browns.

MAKES TWO TO THREE SERVINGS

INDEX